REED HASTINGS

Also by Matt Burgess

Freedom of Information:
A Practical Guide for UK Journalists

REED HASTINGS
Building Netflix

Matt Burgess

W&N
WEIDENFELD & NICOLSON

First published in Great Britain in 2020 by Weidenfeld & Nicolson
an imprint of The Orion Publishing Group Ltd
Carmelite House, 50 Victoria Embankment
London EC4Y 0DZ

An Hachette UK Company

10 9 8 7 6 5 4 3 2 1

ISBN (hardback) 978 1 4746 1254 8
ISBN (ebook) 978 1 4746 1255 5

Typeset by Input Data Services Ltd, Somerset
Printed and bound in Great Britain by Clays Ltd, Elcograf S.p.A.

www.orionbooks.co.uk

CONTENTS

1

CAN ANYONE BEAT REED HASTINGS?

The moment modern television changed for ever can be traced back to one individual day: Tuesday, 16 January 2007. The reasonably sized DVD rental website Netflix, which had gathered around five million subscribers in almost a decade of business, launched a bold new service to its members.

Following in the footsteps of YouTube, Netflix would start beaming video directly to people's computers. But unlike the Google-owned YouTube, the company would stream movies and television shows to PCs, building on its DVD business. Everything was quality content. Shaky handheld homemade cat videos were not included.

For the first time in 100 years of television history it was possible for viewers to pick what they wanted to see and watch it at the exact moment they desired. There would be no lengthy hours spent waiting for a movie to download. It could be streamed instantly. A strict TV schedule detailing when a show would broadcast no longer governed the lives of consumers. (Nor would they need to programme a VHS recorder if they were going to be out at the time a new episode aired.)

With one swift move, Netflix handed the power of television viewing from powerful networks and media conglomerates to the individual. It offered the ultimate flexibility in consumer convenience. Suddenly, it was possible to binge-watch every episode of an entire series back to back. And importantly for Reed Hastings, the charismatic CEO and co-founder of Netflix, it gave his company a distinct advantage over the competition.

The service wasn't perfect by any means. There were only several hundred shows that could be watched over the internet to begin with, the quality was relatively poor, high-speed internet connections were a necessity and viewing was limited to PCs, hardly an ideal position to watch a two-hour-long film.

But six months later Netflix subscribers in the US had watched movies and TV episodes through their computers five million times. An internet television revolution had been started, and the traditional powers within the industry were left flat-footed. Since then, they have been unable to match Netflix's technological offering and lost serious ground to the Californian company.

When Netflix moved into producing its own movies and TV shows five years later, it similarly upended Hollywood.

The company's huge chequebook has allowed it to lavishly buy top talent to star in its shows and hoover up unsigned productions that it has branded as its own. In the process it has won almost every single industry award possible.

Within a few short years, the company has amassed more than 150 million subscribers and is the streaming firm that everyone wants to beat. Now competitors are scrambling to offer their own rival services and draw in their own subscribers. The big question is: can anyone beat Hastings?

Over the last 20 years, Hastings has grown Netflix into one of the internet's most dominant companies. From humble beginnings in a former bank it has grown to more than 5,000 employees spread across global offices, including Hollywood, Los Angeles, London, Amsterdam, Paris, Mexico City and Tokyo. On a single day at the start of 2018, people around the world watched more than 350 million hours of movies, TV shows and documentaries on his platform.

Yet Netflix isn't a new phenomenon. Hastings started the business in 1997 after successfully launching (and subsequently selling) a software development company as part of a deal originally valued at $890m.

When Hastings founded Netflix, many of the technological behemoths that dominate online life today hadn't even been dreamed up. Google launched a year after Netflix, it took another decade before the first iPhone was released, Mark Zuckerberg was just entering his teenage years and half a decade away from launching Facebook (2004) from his Harvard dorm room, Twitter didn't start until 2006, and Uber wasn't founded until 2009.

Netflix started out as an online seller of DVDs and a postal rental service – a business that's radically different to what it is today – but at its core is a simple idea: provide people with entertainment and take up their time on a quiet evening or weekend afternoon.

Currently this takes place in the format of movies, documentaries and TV series being streamed across the internet to televisions, laptops, tablets and smartphones. It used to be solely through DVDs. Since 2007, streaming technology has allowed Netflix customers to pick what they watch, when they watch it and how they watch it. And the service is almost universal.

Netflix streams to more than 190 countries around the world, with operations missing from only a few. It's not available in China (not through lack of trying), the Republic of Crimea in Russia, North Korea or Syria. In July 2019, Netflix had amassed 151 million subscribers, who pay to access its shows and help it to revenues of $4.5bn every three months. There are no ads on the service and more than half of its subscribers live outside the United States.

Since its earliest days, Netflix has operated a subscription model whereby customers pay a small amount every month to access video. At the beginning the subscription prices put limits on the number of discs that could be rented at one time – if you were willing to pay for it you could rent an unlimited number of DVDs in a month.

Now Netflix doesn't set limits to how much a person can

watch – it wants them to spend as much time as possible in its apps and viewing its shows. (Data limits set by mobile service providers may dictate certain restrictions, though.) If you want to watch a stand-up comedy gig at four o'clock in the morning or blast your way through a 12-episode series in one sitting then you can. (During the late 2000s, the company's popularity saw the creation of the Netflix and Chill meme. The phrase became a synonym for inviting a date to a person's house with the underlying assumption that sex could be likely.)

Since 2012, Netflix's business model has evolved from a service that just operates over the internet to one that makes its own video content. It's now no longer a company that solely purchases movies and TV shows from studios. Netflix's catalogue of shows is dominated by its Originals – productions it has purchased the rights to exclusively or, in a growing number of cases, produced itself. The second Netflix Original – *House of Cards*, starring Kevin Spacey – cost Netflix around $100m per series, and by 2018 its overall budget for content had risen to a colossal $12bn and reports claimed it would have more than 1,000 Originals by the start of 2019. The movies and TV series are made in multiple countries around the world, and its shows have seen it scoop up nominations and wins in the Golden Globes, Emmy Awards and the Oscars. For the first time in Netflix's history, in 2018 it was nominated for more Emmy Awards than HBO and in January 2019 it received its first Oscar nomination for the coveted Best Picture award. The title, *Roma*, ultimately did not win.

At the centre of all of Netflix's success has been Hastings. The thoughtful leader has sat at the helm since the business's second year of operations. Initially an engineer who started and sold a software debugging business, Hastings has had to learn how to effectively manage people and grow a company to a global scale.

Hastings has interests in politics and has been an education philanthropist for more than a decade, donating hundreds of millions of dollars to businesses and charities. Yet he is fairly private. His personal and family life are rarely talked about in the press – let alone by him. After decades taking questions from the press, he is now incredibly media polished, although he can be vociferous in his criticism of competitors and politicians he does not agree with. He's battled with Hollywood, legislators, TV executives and their production studios, plus an ever-growing list of rivals.

His former employees credit him with honesty, intelligence and an eagerness to learn, and describe him as a person who values disagreement. They say he takes an analytical approach to decisions, can focus on data, and has the foresight to see future problems before they have arrived. Even during the early DVD-only days of Netflix, Hastings talked about the company's future in downloads and streaming. People spoken to in the reporting for this book say Hastings will often ask them detailed questions about their work that they haven't even considered, despite working on projects for months at a time. He is often one step ahead of all those around him.

Conversely, they say he can often appear to lack empathy

and is highly competitive. During the two decades of Netflix, Hastings and colleagues have struck crucial deals with movie studios, TV broadcasters and hardware firms to promote the company, crucially getting the service in front of more potential subscribers. Some of its shows now get viewerships of tens of millions of people.

'The dream 20 years from now,' Hastings told *WIRED* magazine back in 2002, 'is to have a global entertainment distribution company that provides a unique channel for film producers and studios.'[1] That was achieved before the deadline but it hasn't exactly been a smooth process, with fears for Netflix's survival being a possibility more than once.

His biggest mistake came when he attempted to split the business into two in 2011 – one purely handling streaming and another to deliver DVDs. There was outrage. The split followed a huge 60 per cent price hike for subscribers, and just months after announcing the change Netflix abandoned the idea. In total, 800,000 subscribers deserted the company and its stock dropped by more than 50 per cent.

Unlike Google, Facebook and Twitter, Netflix has seen very few public controversies. Foreign governments haven't been accused of infiltrating its systems, and its lack of advertisements means the data it collects about users is more limited than that gathered by its rivals. That's not to say it hasn't suffered privacy scandals: it cancelled a competition designed for members of the public to improve its recommendation algorithms after it became possible for people to be identified, and it faces regulators around the world that look to control or censor its shows. Like all of Hollywood some of the actors its productions have employed have been accused of sexual harassment or abuse of people they have worked with – the most well-known of whom is Kevin Spacey; it was reported dropping Spacey's projects cost Netflix $39m – as a toxic culture reigned supreme across the movie business.

Perhaps Hastings's biggest success at Netflix has been being able to ensure the company has survived. Its stock has consistently fluctuated as investors have speculated on which competitor may knock it out of business. During the mid-2000s Netflix fought an intense price war with Blockbuster as it looked to convert its failing physical rental stores into a flourishing digital business and catch up with Hastings's lead.

While Netflix beat Blockbuster, the streaming age has introduced new competitors. Amazon has its Prime Video service, Disney has Disney+ and is in the process pulling its content from Netflix, Apple has its TV+ service, YouTube is increasingly moving towards highly produced programmatic videos, and there is the omnipresent threat of Hulu and HBO. Each of these competitors has prompted analysts to seriously question whether Netflix can survive in an increasingly saturated digital environment, and as a result its stock has seen occasional, short-term, dips in value.

But, for the time being at least, Hastings does not see any of them as his major competition. He believes there's a place for multiple streaming companies and what will stop them all from growing is customers spending time on other activities that aren't sitting in front of a screen. 'You know, think about it, when you watch a show from Netflix and you get addicted to it, you stay up late at night,' he told investors on an earnings call in April 2017. 'We're competing with sleep, on the margin. And so, it's a very large pool of time.'

2

REED HASTINGS JR

Wilmot Reed Hastings Jr was born on 8 October 1960, in Massachusetts, United States. As the son of Joan Amory and Wilmot Reed Hastings, he grew up in the relatively well-off neighbourhood of Belmont, a suburb that's around a 30-minute drive from the state's capital city, Boston.

His father served as a lawyer for the US government, working for the Department of Health, Education and Welfare during the Nixon administration. But his mother's side of the family has a history of technology, innovation and engineering that would ultimately trickle down to the Netflix co-founder.

His great-grandfather was the inventor and scientist Alfred Lee Loomis. When he died, aged 87 in 1975, the *New York Times* called him a 'renowned' physicist.[1] Loomis is credited with helping to develop techniques for electroencephalography (EEG), which is used for brain scans, and the long-range navigation system, LORAN, which was used by the United States in the Second World War; he also worked as a lawyer and helped to found the research group, the RAND Corporation.

Hastings lives in Santa Cruz with his wife, Patty Ann Quillin, and the pair have two children. The family has kept a number of pets over the years, owning at one point four shelter dogs, ten chickens and four goats, including Nigerian dwarf goats (a type of goat that's relatively easy to keep as a pet and pretty small in stature).

For most of his professional life Hastings has sported a greying goatee and had a laid-back demeanour, and in public appearances usually wears dark jeans, a shirt and a suit jacket. In the early days of Netflix he was often found in khaki shorts, sandals and T-shirts: the uniform of Silicon Valley.

When speaking publicly and to the press, Hastings is generally open. He attempts to answer most questions that are directed at him in a way that seems to be honest. The answers he gives to questions can take two forms: he repeats the line of questioning before answering; or he can use a number of go-to anecdotes that have been repeated multiple times.

In keeping with this, his personal life is largely kept private. In 2014 he told the *New Yorker* he wasn't that exciting – either out of a desire to keep it completely quiet or because it genuinely is the case. 'Unfortunately, and weirdly, I have almost no hobbies,' Hastings told the publication. 'I don't sail, I don't fish. I'm a pitiful failure as a Renaissance man.'[2]

In 2012, he admitted to *Vanity Fair* magazine that he doesn't particularly enjoy being a figurehead in public life. He'd rather largely remain private. 'It's an appropriate and necessary sacrifice,' he said. 'But, on a personal basis, it's pure downside, because then you just get more recognised. You lead a less normal life. I hate the photo shoots. I hate all that stuff.'[3] Despite the professional necessity of his having a public profile, it's unlikely many people would recognise Hastings in the same way Mark Zuckerberg is known.

Hastings entered the *Forbes* list of the top 400 wealthiest people in the US – all of them billionaires – for the first time in 2017.[4] A year later he had climbed from around 350th to 215th in the list, and with Netflix's strong financial performance it's likely he will climb even higher. As of April 2019, Bloomberg's Billionaires Index list places Hastings at 427 and says his $4.57bn net worth could buy 63.8 million barrels of crude oil.[5]

Although he has been a billionaire for some time now, Hastings generally isn't a flashy man. He doesn't overtly – unlike some other tech billionaires – show his wealth and status. He learnt a valuable lesson early on in his career. After selling his first company, Hastings took part in an interview with the newspaper *USA Today* for an article on the ever-increasing number of millionaires in Silicon Valley. The subsequent write-up resulted in a picture of Hastings lounging on the bonnet of his brand-new Porsche Carrera being splashed on the front page of the paper. The caption? 'Boom! You are rich!'

He went to Buckingham Browne & Nichols School, which is not far from Belmont or Harvard University. The establishment is a private school whose roots go back to the late 1800s. Hastings graduated in 1978, four years after it became mixed sex.

He was interested in going to college and ended up at the liberal arts establishment Bowdoin, a hundred miles north of Boston on the East Coast. But he didn't rush straight into his maths major at the college and instead took a year out to continue working in his first job of selling Rainbow vacuum cleaners door to door around Boston. In a 2015 talk he said the experience was a 'fantastic introduction to selling'.[6] He's also said he loved the job as he met plenty of different people. 'As a sales pitch, I cleaned the carpet with the vacuum the customer had and then cleaned it with the Rainbow,' he said in a *New York Times* column, 'The Boss', in 2006.[7]

The early selling experience didn't stop him attending Bowdoin and getting his bachelor's degree. During his time at the college he excelled in maths – something that would later be useful during the development of artificial intelligence systems. Bill Barker, one of Hastings's former teachers, told the college's university newspaper that Hastings had 'confidence without arrogance'.[8] At the college Hastings ran the Outing Club, an adventure and outdoors club for which he organised climbing and canoeing trips, among other activities.

Before he graduated from Bowdoin in 1983, Hastings spent a semester at the University of Bath, in the UK, and another summer training at a Marine Corps boot camp. He had intended to go into the service but the summer was a misplaced one. He wasn't suited to a regimented and disciplined life in the Marines – he told an education publication in 2015: 'I'm not good at following orders.'[9] Instead he opted for the softer Peace Corps, a voluntary programme run by the US government that's designed to help provide social and economic support to other countries.

Here Hastings was assigned to a teaching job. He spent three years teaching maths in Eswatini, which was known as Swaziland at the time.

During his time in the country, Hastings enjoyed the lifestyle and culture change. He experienced the outdoors and made the most of being able to travel through the country's vast landscapes. Not forgetting his old mathematics teacher, Bill Barker, Hastings wrote letters to him while he was there. Details of these were reported by the *Bowdoin Orient* student newspaper years later.

'The first year I loved,' he wrote. Hastings said he lived with a family around three kilometres from the school he taught at and walked to and from work. 'The second year I lived at the school with the other teachers and spent my afternoons playing cards and drinking beer.'

In other letters he is said to have written that he didn't feel particularly challenged by the time he was spending there. ('I would never dribble away my days at home like this,' he is said to have written.) The student newspaper wrote that his innovative flair first started to show itself during these slower periods. 'The answer to my boredom and under-utilization was to get involved with the community as a whole instead of limiting myself to the school compound.'

He started to create a plan to build a tank on top of the village's hill so rainwater could be collected where it was needed, and he also requested money from the United States so people could start beekeeping. After being granted the money Hastings helped to teach courses on building beehives and looking after the insects, the student newspaper wrote.[10]

It was during this time that Hastings started to consider what he would do next. 'I didn't want to be math professor, it seemed just too dry,' he said during a 2015 talk at an investment firm, Kleiner Perkins Caufield & Byers.[11] Instead, after around three years in Africa he settled on studying on a course involving a huge maths element but also one that incorporated computers.

During the early 1980s, the field of artificial intelligence was going through its second boom. After emerging during the 1960s, the principles of using algorithms to solve computer problems had died away: a lack of processing power limited its progress. But by the time Hastings was mulling over his future there was a renewed faith in AI with the development of the 'expert system'. The programs were designed to use a large base of knowledge to find answers to potential real-world problems. During the decade, the systems became hugely popular within universities and at large *Fortune* 500 companies that wanted to take advantage of computer-aided decisions.

Hastings joined this boom and applied to study at the renowned Massachusetts Institute of Technology (MIT), just a few miles from the Boston suburbs where he had grown up. He also applied to the West Coast's Stanford University. 'It's not a huge surprise because I didn't have any computer science background, but I didn't get into MIT,' he said in the 2015 talk. However, Stanford did let him on to its course.

The trip to Stanford was the first time Hastings had ever travelled to the west of the US. He called himself naive to the state's laid-back culture and straightforward way of life. He told the *New York Times*: 'Driving up to the campus I saw palm trees. It was dry and brown. I asked myself, "Where's the ivy?" Within a week I had fallen in love with California.'[12]

The Stanford AI course was the start of his time in technology, and Hastings relished it. 'When I came back [from Eswatini] I really got into computers,' he told a technology website, *The Next Web*, in 2013. 'At Stanford in the AI program, and for the next couple of years, I just programmed, and it was just such a joy I couldn't even imagine doing this as a job as opposed to a hobby. It was just such a joy to develop things.'[13]

From this point, his future in technology was almost assured – he briefly dabbled in politics before Netflix – but a spark for entrepreneurialism had been created. He thrived on competition and creating new products that people could use. After graduating from Stanford in 1988 Hastings bounced around between a few different roles, evidently struggling to find the exact satisfaction and calling he wanted. First he worked in the research division of the oilfield giant Schlumberger, and then moved to an artificial intelligence startup, Coherent Thought, which suffered the ill fate of the 1980s AI bubble bursting.

Things started to change for Hastings when he joined Adaptive Technology. The company, founded by the entrepreneur and investor Audrey MacLean, was spun out from (and later merged with) Network Equipment Technologies and built high-speed switches for computer networks. Hastings was employed as a software engineer and it was here he formed the idea for his first business.

Bugs in the code

Raymond Peck first met Reed Hastings at a party and didn't know what it would lead to. Sometime in the late 1980s, Peck's girlfriend was working at Coherent Thought, the same artificial intelligence startup where Hastings was a software engineer. Through the company's weekly Friday beer bashes, Peck, an engineer by trade, started to get to know Hastings.

'He was a very happy guy. Not goofy, kind of reserved, but very cordial and warm,' Peck recalls during a Skype conversation. 'Not at all your stereotypical software guy, he had a lot of charisma even at that time – he just had a lot of magnetism to him.'

Even though it was the first time they had met, Peck knew

of Hastings before they started to share beers. He was at Stanford at the same time as Hastings but on a different course. Peck says he was responsible for grading some basic programming language class papers at Stanford. In only one of the 100 papers he marked one year did the author really know what they were talking about: it was Hastings. He was already impressed by his knowledge.

It was at the Friday afternoon company parties when the two of them started talking about Hastings's idea for a new software tool called Purify. Hastings was looking for someone who could help write the underlying code to make Purify work and it was exactly the sort of job that Peck knew how to do. 'In the summer of '91 we started working on it together,' Peck says. 'He had the code partially working, kind of handed it over to me, and he disappeared off to Europe for the summer.' Over the next six months the pair worked on the code together, with Peck eventually deciding to quit his full-time job to work for the newly formed company, Pure Software.

Pure Software's first office was in Los Altos, somewhere between San Jose and San Francisco, and five employees made up the initial roster. Hastings was the CEO and Peck was considered as co-founder. He says that during the company's earliest days Hastings paid for a professional photographer to visit the office and take photos of the group – Hastings was already planning for success and Pure's potential legacy.

The premise of the company was simple: create a tool that would tell software developers when there were errors in the code they were writing. The result, which like all good ideas was more complex to execute than the initial thought, was Purify.

The programming language C was wildly popular at the start of the 1990s. The code, which is still used today and forms the basis of other programming techniques, allows people to write software in a relatively simple way and works across a litany of operating systems. C also gave birth to the C++ programming language that is used in web browsers, operating systems and video games.

Purify aimed to cut out the errors developers were creating within C and C++. Mistakes left in the code of software, particularly around a program's memory usage, can cause unpredictability and slowness, and in the most extreme cases they can crash a computer. 'It is nearly impossible to eliminate all such errors from a non-trivial program,' Hastings wrote in a technical paper outlining how Purify worked. 'Purify provides nearly-comprehensive memory access checking and memory leak detection,' the paper said. He called the automated system a 'safety net' that didn't 'impair the ultimate performance'.[14]

The promise of Purify was that it would help software developers remove bugs faster from their systems than if they manually had to check all of their code. In turn they, and the companies they worked for, would be able to launch their products to customers faster. An advertisement run in the technology magazine *CIO* in 1996 said Pure's tools would let software development 'become more predictable and easier to manage'.[15]

Peck, who had been working in components and hardware before helping to found Pure, says Hastings had amazingly high standards on quality and a vision of what the product should be. 'What was really strong from the very beginning was his very extreme pursuit of excellence and making customers just unbelievably happy,' he recalls. 'And, you know, driving quality to the highest degree possible. The emphasis on quality that Reed had from the beginning was higher than what we did in hardware,' he adds.

Purify was Pure Software's first product, but despite its usefulness it wasn't easy for Hastings to bring it to market. He had started the company with Peck and Mark Box in 1991. Before this, sometime around 1990, Hastings approached his boss, Audrey MacLean, at Adaptive Technology with his idea for Purify. She was keen on the product and the idea, but Hastings's approaches to venture capitalists had already failed.

MacLean, along with a group of other backers, including Hastings's friends and family, all invested $20,000 each to get the company started. Her role was instrumental. In a *Forbes* article in 1998 Hastings said MacLean has been 'a hard-ass coach who draws the best out of people', adding that she was 'brutally honest' with him.[16] As the product started to come together, MacLean took a seat on the Pure board and helped raise an extra $6.4m in funding.

The company had a successful few initial years. It launched an entire suite of software checking tools: PureVision, PureDDTS, PureTestExpert, PurePerformix,

PureCoverage and Quantify. All of these were designed to make developers' lives easier. Despite its rapid growth Hastings has said he struggled with hiring the right people to take the business forward over the long term – staff turnover was high.

'I changed our VP of sales every year for five years in a row, I just couldn't pick,' Hastings said during a talk at Kleiner Perkins Caufield & Byers in 2015. 'I kept picking the wrong sort of person. I just didn't know that much.'[17] Peck remembers there being a quick turnover at the vice-president level in the company as Hastings had exceptionally high standards and excitement about the products that were being made. 'They just didn't get it,' Peck says. 'They didn't understand what made Pure great.'

Hastings has said that during his time at Pure he hadn't set out to be in charge of the company. He was a product person at heart and cared more about his creation and the other tools the business made than he did his management style. In 2010 *Fortune* reported that Hastings had been given the nickname 'Animal' during his time leading Pure. The publication also said that the culture at Pure made it a difficult place to work and that meetings would be filled with arguments. ('We were all young and didn't know any better,' Hastings said in response.)[18]

Being in charge of a company that grew so quickly gave Hastings a chance to learn and understand how to work with other people below him within a business. It was his first experience of management. 'Every year there were twice as many people and it was trial by fire,' he told *Inc* in 2005. 'I was underprepared for the complexities and personalities.'[19]

'We grew very quickly, but very chaotically,' Hastings said on stage at the TechFest event run by the *New Yorker* magazine in October 2016. 'I was uncomfortable about being honest with people so I valued kindness very high, and consideration,' he said. 'I'd be frustrated with you but I wouldn't really tell you, but it would, of course, manifest itself, and it took me a long time to have the courage both to be able to be an example of honesty myself and to receive it.'[20]

Hastings has also said, in a 2011 interview with *Venturebeat*, that he was trying to do too much at Pure. He was coding in the night and trying to manage people during the day. This took a toll on his personal life. 'My marriage counsellor became a great CEO coach and mentor. He forced me to admit that I cared more about the success of the business than the marriage,' he told the publication.[21]

Peck says that until the company employed more than around 50 or 60 people, Hastings was much more involved with the engineering teams. 'It was about him transmitting his idea of what the culture should be, and making sure that everybody was excited and injecting energy into the group,' he says. Following a similar pattern in other start-ups, as the company grew its culture started to change, as did Hastings's influence over all of the operations. Peck says: 'Definitely it got diluted. And, you know, I definitely lay that at least partially on him.'

But in 1995 the company was nearing 600 employees and

Hastings was ready to take it public. It had already bought a number of its competitors, and at the start of August, around the same time the dotcom bubble was starting to rise, Pure held its IPO (Initial Public Offering), organised by Morgan Stanley. The company offered two million shares and current shareholders sold up to 750,000 shares. Pure was set to raise $31m in proceeds that it would use as capital and to help fund its future growth.

After the company went public, things started to get messy. Less than a year after the IPO, Hastings struck a deal to buy a fellow software management tool firm, Atria Software. The deal took place as a stock swap and was initially valued at around $928m (by the time it was completed this had dropped to a valuation of $623m). Atria had built tools that allowed developers to keep track of changes that were being made to code and to manage the work of multiple coders at once. After the deal Pure Software became the Pure Atria Corporation, with headquarters in Sunnyvale, California, and Hastings would be president and CEO of the company, with Paul Levine (the CEO of Atria Software) taking the role of chairman.

As the company matured Hastings has said it became less fun to work at. Hastings has said he struggled so much running the business that he tried to resign. Twice. On multiple occasions Hastings has publicly said he felt like he was underwater and drowning while at Pure, and approached the board to say it should fire him.

He has explained that too many processes and procedures were implemented. Each time a mistake was made, a new system to avoid the same error being made again was introduced and this ultimately meant the firm's focus was narrow. It wasn't able to innovate and change its product quickly to meet the demands of a rapidly evolving market.

'We got bought by our largest competitor in 1997 after missing our numbers,' Hastings said in 2015. 'It was a soft landing to what would have been very bad news.'[22] At the time, the programming industry was starting to move away from C and C++, focusing instead on the new Java language. This shrunk the appetite for Pure's products, which weren't compatible with the new way of programming.

In April that year Rational Software announced that it was to buy Hastings's business in a deal that was set to be worth around $900m. Rational, which itself was later purchased by IBM, was Pure's biggest competitor and the market leader in software automation. By the time the deal was completed later that year, it made Hastings a wealthy man: the sale was completed around the $750m mark. However, it was the beginning of the end for Hastings's time in software development.

How Rational was run did teach Hastings a final lesson, though. 'It was so different how they operated – the level of trust and the quality of interaction between them was impressive,' Hastings told *Fortune*. 'That gave me a North Star, something I wanted to grow toward.'[23] (At Netflix the phrase 'North Star' is often used for people's ambitions and the direction that they want to head in.)

Peck says: 'The idea was that because they were almost our equal in size, there would kind of be two headquarters, but the cultures of the company couldn't have been more different.' Hastings didn't see the sale as a victory. At a media conference in Berlin in 2015 he said: 'I was very disappointed because I was so ego-identified in my own eyes with the company and what we did that I felt like a failure.'[24]

As well as the money, which helped Hastings to fund Netflix, he also hired and worked with a lot of the people he would later employ at the entertainment company. Many of the key employees at Pure followed Hastings to his next venture and worked in senior roles during its formative years. In many ways he considers the end of Pure as a second chance to be a CEO – although he did consider a few other careers before working full-time at Netflix. 'For me, it is redemption because I got to start over as a CEO. In the first company, I was a very good product person but not a good CEO. I was not a great CEO. In the second company, as you get to start over, I was much more thoughtful.'[25]

3

THE BIRTH OF NETFLIX

The date 11 April 1970 was a historic day. At around 14.13 the engines of the Apollo 13 rocket ignited, lifting the giant spacecraft off the ground, through the Earth's atmosphere, and starting it on a 384,400 km journey to the moon. But onboard the craft attempting to put humans on our nearest satellite for the third time, not everything was going smoothly.

Two days into the crew's mission, long before reaching their destination, an oxygen tank onboard exploded and damaged key technical equipment. Scrambling to save their lives, the three astronauts piloting the craft were forced to change plans: instead orbiting the moon and completing daring manoeuvres to return to Earth safely.

The doomed mission has been well documented – most successfully in the theatrical *Apollo 13* movie released in

1995 and directed by Ron Howard, with Tom Hanks and Kevin Bacon playing leading roles. And shortly after it was released to the public, Hastings wanted to watch it.

Sometime before 1997 he rented the movie on VHS but lost the tape. The video was around six weeks overdue and racking up penalty charges for not being returned on time. Hastings has said the video store he rented it from was owed around $40 in fees and he was feeling guilty. 'I didn't want to tell my wife about it,' he wrote in the *New York Times* in 2002. 'And I said to myself, "I'm going to compromise the integrity of my marriage over a late fee?"'[1]

Around the same time, he was travelling to the gym and started thinking about how it made money: one monthly payment allowed for as much exercise as a person could stomach. So why couldn't this apply to movies as well?

These two events have been key ingredients in Hastings's story of how Netflix was started. He has repeated them multiple times during Netflix's 20-year history. However, it isn't the full picture (and it's possible they may never even have happened at all). Howard's depiction of Apollo 13 falls into the genre of a docudrama: something that's based on real-world events but embellishes the finer details to have the greatest impact. It's likely that Netflix's origin story falls into the same genre.

Hastings has also credited a computer science course he took at Stanford University as a third inspiration for the birth of the company. In the anecdote he says the class leader set students thinking about a problem in which they had to calculate the bandwidth of a station wagon carrying tapes across the United States. The result is a distribution network that's able to carry huge amounts of data at once. The station wagon was replaced by Netflix's red DVD-carrying envelopes and then, eventually, the internet.

Hastings wasn't the only founder at Netflix: he created the company with Marc Randolph. Coming from a marketing background, Randolph was the company's first CEO and was responsible for a huge amount of the business's direction between its incorporation in August 1997 – the company was first registered under the name Kibble – and the launch of the first Netflix DVD delivery service around a year later. (He left in 2002 after Hastings had become CEO.)

Randolph's story of how the company was born is slightly different to Hastings's – and it's one that's likely to hold more truth. Plenty of tech founders, including those from eBay and Google, have embellished the boring stories of how their companies came to be. And it probably shouldn't come as a surprise that having a compelling, media-friendly origin story has helped companies get their name recognised.

Randolph and Hastings worked together at Pure Software before they founded Netflix, and it was in the quiet months when Pure was being acquired by Rational when thoughts turned to a new business. At the time the pair used to car-pool to Pure's offices, and as they did so they discussed possible new ventures. The undertone to many of the conversations, Randolph recalled in an interview with the *Silicon Valley Business Journal* in 2014, was about the dominance of Amazon. Jeff Bezos had launched the online retailer as a bookstore in July 1994 and the business was burgeoning. As many entrepreneurs do, the car-pooling pair turned to imitation: 'Can we create an Amazon for X.' (More than a decade later the phenomenon would be repeated in creating an 'Uber for X'.)

Randolph said he and Hastings mulled over the idea of creating an online VHS rental platform but decided against the plan as the tapes cost too much and it would almost be impossible to take on the dominant Blockbuster in its own market. Thankfully, the giant had a weakness. Hastings and Randolph had just heard of a new video format that was being tested: DVD. The CD-style discs were still experimental but they could hold a huge amount of data, were lightweight, and if they were embraced by movie studios and retailers they had the potential to be the next iteration of home movie viewing.

They decided to experiment, but didn't have a single DVD because the trials were so limited. 'One of the founding myth stories that is actually very true is the fact that Reed and I did go down to Logo's in Santa Cruz and bought a used CD, and then went to one of the little gift shop stores on Pacific Avenue,' Randolph told the *Business Journal*. 'We bought ourselves one of those little blue envelopes that you put the greeting cards in and we mailed a CD to Reed's house.'

The experiment worked. The DVD arrived at Hastings's home unscathed a couple of days later. As Randolph described it: 'That was the moment where the two of us looked at each other and said: "This idea just might work."[2] The concept was born and the two agreed that Randolph would lead a new company that posted DVDs to customers. At the start, Hastings was to back the new business with financial investment and be part of its board, while Randolph acted as CEO.

One monthly fee

The Netflix we have today is incomparable to the business that launched on 14 April 1998. Hastings's venture capital funding had helped to hire around 30 employees, who built the company's website, acquired DVDs, and created an unsophisticated distribution system in around a year. His money also helped house the company in an old bank, which was converted to an office. Its vault was the first location of Netflix's DVD collection.

The business – stylised as NetFlix – started off selling and renting DVDs through its website and the whole setup was very bare bones. The company called itself the 'world's first Internet store to offer DVD rentals'. But as DVDs were such a rare thing the official company announcement had to explain what the disc was and what the benefits would be for consumers. Nobody had heard of DVDs at this point, and the number of people who owned players was even smaller.

Netflix stocked just 900 DVD titles when it launched but, showing how the format really was in its infancy, this was almost every movie that was on DVD at the time. Initially, customers logged on to the netflix.com website and could rent, buy or reserve DVDs that were then added to their carts. One of the limited number of features on the site at its launch time was 'FlixFinder' – a search system that was essentially a database of the titles it stocked, actors who were in movies and the directors behind them.

The company promised same-day shipping, with DVDs arriving in the post two or three days after an order had been made (providing the title was in stock). Customers could keep a DVD for seven days before late fees started to accumulate and two DVDs could be rented for $4 each at the same time. (A $2 handling fee was also applied for the first disc in any order.) One additional rental feature was the option for a customer to keep the DVD they had just watched. Sending an email to Netflix saying the DVD was going to be kept would charge the customer the buying price (minus what they had already paid for rental).

Six months after Netflix launched it had managed to more than double the number of DVDs it offered to potential customers, reaching the 2,000 mark in September 1998. However, at this time, Hastings's main focus wasn't on the company. In June 1998, a lobbying group called The Technology Network (TechNet for short) had named him as its new president.

The organisation was launched the year before, based in Palo Alto, and was created to help Silicon Valley's leaders to get access to politicians and to lobby lawmakers – key campaign issues were around foreign visa quotas, education changes and securities reform. Hastings's tenure as president was short-lived. He stepped down as leader around six months after joining, saying he had to focus more on his role at Netflix.

It was 1999 when Hastings replaced Randolph as Netflix's CEO. Mitch Lowe, a vice-president at the company who worked in the role from 1998, says in an interview that the change partly happened because the deals Netflix struck to have vouchers put inside the boxes of DVD manufacturers was found to have a flaw and Hastings, who had been paying for the company's operations, would have been liable for it. Lowe says: 'We had not thought through fraud prevention, like photocopying the barcode, or one per customer. So we had, and I can't remember the exact amount, but, well, more than a million dollars' worth of fraud of people submitting demands for movies that were basically duplicates, multiple people, submitting multiple forms, and we have not created the way to stop that from happening.'

Despite this, the company had started to see some growth, and with this excitement Hastings had become more involved with the business and started visiting the office more frequently. Randolph, discussing his move from CEO with the *Silicon Valley Business Journal*, said he believed Hastings's interest in Netflix was piqued because of its initial promise, and the fact that he missed being an entrepreneur and being involved in growing a company. There were intense discussions around whether Hastings should join the team full-time.

'As I look back on what some of the smartest things I ever did at Netflix [were], I think having him come back and be a very, very major part of the company, eventually becoming CEO in my place, was probably the smartest thing I ever did there,' Randolph said, crediting Hastings's ability to spot problems at an early stage and solve them creatively.[3]

Perhaps one of the most important decisions in Hastings's and Netflix's history was the choice to stop charging for individual rentals. The subscription model – which was allegedly inspired by *Apollo 13* and the visit to the gym – was called the Marquee programme in December 1999. It was one of the first big announcements Netflix made with Hastings's name as CEO against it.

To this day, Netflix still relies on subscribers for its revenue, and of the big, dominant tech firms only Amazon's Prime service (which has its own Netflix streaming rival as well as faster shopping delivery) utilises a paid-subscription service. Google's, Facebook's and Apple's wealth comes from advertising and hardware sales.

Hastings started the Marquee programme to stand out, particularly to Blockbuster. The scheme scrapped due dates for rented DVDs to be returned and with them late fees also vanished (before this, the one-week rental period had been increased to two weeks). For $15.95 per month, which could be cancelled at any time (something relatively unheard of for contracts then), customers were able to rent four DVDs per month and return the discs in Netflix's prepaid envelope once they had watched them.

The Marquee programme also introduced a piece of tech that Netflix would later call the queue. It would prove invaluable to the company's growth during its DVD age and was technically a product that helped it to overcome Blockbuster. Quite simply, the queue was a list of movies that customers wanted to see. The Netflix website allowed titles to be added to a list and when they were in stock they would be mailed out. For the consumer it was an automatic, almost unconscious way to be sent films they wanted to watch.

The queue's potential power, however, didn't start to develop until a month later, when Cinematch was launched. Although relatively rudimentary, Cinematch was Netflix's first recommendation algorithm that attempted to match users up with films and shows they would be interested in watching, but hadn't heard of. Hastings said it would provide 'personalised movie recommendations that are based upon an individual's own tastes'.

Netflix's algorithm has become one of its unique selling points – attempting to predict viewing habits and provide people with shows they'd enjoy watching. Like all good algorithms, Cinematch's one needed user data to base its recommendations on. Customers were asked to rate 20 or more movies, giving them a rating out of five stars. These recommendations would see them grouped into categories whereby they would then be presented with choices that might appeal to them.

While Cinematch provided a way for users to hone their tastes, its real advantage was what it allowed Netflix to do with its ever-expanding catalogue of DVDs. In early 2000, the company had around 5,200 DVD titles in its collection. Naturally, some of these would be more popular than others and customers generally wanted to watch the biggest movies as soon as they could.

However, the recommendation engine allowed smaller, lesser-known movies to be pushed in the direction of subscribers who might be interested in watching them but never would have found, or picked, them organically. Keeping the DVD collection circulating allowed customers to always be receiving movies and helped to stem availability issues when there was a high demand for a small number of big titles.

Tom Dillon, Netflix's chief operations officer between 1999 and 2006, oversaw the firm's shipping business. In a phone call he describes Hastings as being the 'smartest guy I ever worked for' and says the company's early attitude made it a fun place to work. 'I ran a little warehouse of about 20–25 people [at the beginning], my wife used to come in and help us ship on weekends and things like that,' he says in an interview. By the time he left half a decade later the company shipped more than one million discs a day. He says Netflix was run with precision. 'Everything is measured, everything is looked at and everything you're measuring is supposed to go up or down.'

The early years under Hastings's and Randolph's leadership set the precedent for what was to come. The company would focus on developing its own technology and partnering with external companies to give it a boost into newer markets. In 1998, Netflix struck a deal with Amazon whereby Bezos's company would point people towards rentals at Netflix and, in return, Hastings's website would say DVDs could be purchased from Amazon.

As much as Netflix had a huge DVD collection and the technology to promote its niche titles, it still faced a bigger problem – one that affected every company in the DVD market. Players were massively expensive and not many people owned them. People weren't flocking to buy the devices when they were first released. VHS tapes were popular and didn't die an immediate death. When they were first introduced, DVD players cost around $1,000. The key for Hastings to get around this was through partnerships.

By mid-1999 Netflix had struck deals with the key hardware manufacturers: Panasonic, Philips, Sharp, JVC, Kenwood, Mitsubishi, Marantz, Sony, Toshiba, Pioneer and more. It had also raised $30m of investment from Group Arnault, the investment firm of Bernard Arnault, the chairman and CEO of luxury conglomerate LVMH.

As a new DVD player box opened, out would fall a Netflix advertising flyer giving people free DVD rentals. The promotions gave Hastings's firm captive eyeballs of their key market, and although it led to higher than desired churn rates (customers joining for a short period then leaving the service) it helped to spread the name of the company. One other similar deal saw Netflix work with Circuit City, an electronics retailer, to give away 13 free Netflix rentals when people purchased a DVD player from one of the stores.

On the odd occasion, the company also decided to tap into public sentiment around national events. Straight after

President Bill Clinton gave evidence to a grand jury about his affair with Monica Lewinsky, Netflix started touting a DVD of the proceedings. Netflix sold around 2,000 copies of the disc for $9.95 each before sensing a marketing opportunity: it then charged just two cents (plus shipping) to view it.

The combined efforts of technology, more than 11,000 titles in its collection and a boom in DVD player sales started to pay dividends. Netflix hit 500,000 subscribers in early 2002 and the time appeared right for Hastings to take the company public.

Going public

In the five years leading up to the Millennium, if you wanted to make money from technology all you needed to do in Silicon Valley was have an idea and create a startup. Internet penetration was growing and investors wanted to make money from the dotcom revolution.

Netscape held its initial public offering in August 1995, Yahoo! followed in 1996, and the following two years saw Amazon and eBay hold their own IPOs. Each raised millions of dollars and saw their share prices soar. As money flowed through the companies, the US stock market responded and new entrepreneurs made the most of the chance to get rich. Businesses spent heavily to build large market shares and those with dotcom names found it simple to raise venture capital to fund their growth.

Anyone could have some initial success. In November 1998, Pets.com was introduced to the world. Supported by a knitted, microphone-wielding dog mascot sock puppet, the company raised more than $300m to let people buy pet food online and have it delivered to their homes. The company purchased competitors and hired hundreds of people during a spell of expansion. And backed by extortionate sums of money, the sock puppet went everywhere: it had its own Super Bowl ad, and appeared in the Macy's Parade and on TV shows.

However, the dotcom bubble, like all market fluctuations, popped. On 10 March 2000, the Nasdaq index hit an all-time high. Its value had soared more than 400 per cent in the years beforehand. The market came crashing down as Japan announced it had entered a recession, talks to merge Yahoo! and eBay unsuccessfully ended, and Microsoft lost an anti-competition lawsuit against the US government.

A few months later, by November 2000, the time of Pets.com was up. The company went bust and made around 300 employees redundant. Similarly, a grocery delivery service, Webvan, which had raised almost $800m in venture capital and went public in 1999, collapsed in 2001. The economic crisis that followed the dotcom bubble continued until around the end of 2002.

And while Netflix was growing, it wasn't financially successful. Struggling to turn a profit in 2001 the company cut around a third of its 120 staff. 'It was brutal,' Netflix's former HR director, Patty McCord, wrote in a 2014 *Harvard Business Review* article.[4] The cuts were implemented to make the business more efficient and more likely to make a profit. Later, in her book, *Powerful*, McCord wrote that the company was 'on the brink of bankruptcy'.

In 2016, Hastings recalled worries that Netflix would 'grind to a halt' as he had made so many people jobless. 'In fact, we got more done with only 80 people,' he said. 'We tried to figure out why and we realised now there was no dummy proofing necessary. Everybody was just going fast and everything was right.'[5] In *Powerful*, McCord wrote: 'It taught us that the best thing you can do for employees is hire only high performers to work alongside them.'[6]

Over the first three months of 2002 Hastings's teams saw more than $30m in sales, and a subscriber count of more than 600,000 people, but it wasn't turning a profit. Those months saw it make a net loss of $4.5m, and in the four years since it started operating total losses had hit around $91m.

So when Hastings decided to take Netflix public in 2002, it was a gamble. He'd originally wanted to list the business on the stock markets earlier, but the combination of the dotcom bubble bursting and the September 11 terror attacks against the World Trade Center and the Pentagon had led him to delay the move. Several months later, and despite a successful $61m IPO from PayPal, confidence in the market was still decidedly low.

The gamble, nevertheless, worked. There was enough confidence to see Netflix's vision. On 22 May 2002, Hastings announced he would offer 5,500,000 shares of its common stock with a target range of $13–$15. TV footage from the day showed Netflix employees, some wearing red Netflix jackets and accompanied by a dog wearing a company-branded T-shirt, celebrating as stock markets opened. There was no extortionately high buying rate, with the entire range of stocks being sold at the higher end, $15 per share, raising the company $82.5m. (In comparison, Google's IPO two years later – when it was six years old, was making profits and had billions in revenue – made it $23bn.)

With the IPO secured, confidence within the company was high. Shortly after going public, Michael Ramsay joined the firm's board of directors. Ramsay co-founded and acted as CEO of TiVo, the firm that lets users record TV on to a hard drive to watch later. 'He [Hastings] approached everything with a high degree of confidence, he knew what he wanted to do and he knew what he was doing, and he had the right people to make it happen,' Ramsay said in a phone interview. 'You felt like there was a real team there and the people wanted to follow him as a leader.'

Ramsay says the board met roughly once per month and was confident in the CEO. The pair discussed the media industry and how it was shifting. During the board meetings everything was talked about in detail, he recalls, without there being a 'committee structure' to the proceedings.

Importantly, Hastings knew how to keep the board on his side – there were few conflicts and everyone on it supported his decisions. 'One of the things that keeps board members engaged is if you avoid too much number crunching and detailed analysis and you do more strategy and free thinking,' Ramsay says. 'I think Reed has a good balance of that. So the board meetings were entertaining and informative, and kind of got through the numbers relatively quickly.' (He left the board in 2004 after Netflix and TiVo signed an agreement, which seemingly came to nothing, to work together on technology behind a movie-downloading service.)

At the time, and since, Hastings has warned that taking Netflix public was just the beginning. It would have to use the capital raised wisely if it was going to grow and survive. He learnt what it was like to take a company public with Pure (with a starting price of $17 per share) and, most importantly, what comes next.

'It's kind of like being a virgin and, until you are not, you can't stop thinking about it,' Hastings said of taking companies public, while giving a talk at the Utah Technology Council in 2018. 'Then you get public and you can start to learn what sex is really about. There's a lot to learn and you have to get through that. Then you can start the real learning process of how to try and operate at scale, which is really fun.'[7]

A giant looms

David Cook changed everything. He was a quiet, private man from Dallas, Texas – once admitting he liked dealing with computers more than with people – who created a new software database for oil companies. But when the oil industry suffered a downturn in the early 1980s, business dried up and he turned his attention to another problem: video stores.

On 19 October 1985, Cook opened the first Blockbuster Entertainment store on the corners of Skillman Street and Northwest Highway in Dallas. The shop started with around 8,000 individual titles on Betamax tapes and was an instant success. 'The first night we were so mobbed we had to lock the doors to prevent more people from coming in,' Cook told CNN in 2003.[8] Its system of using electronic barcodes, something we take for granted now, allowed staff to easily monitor the tapes it was renting.

Cook quickly opened new stores around his local area, and when 20 stores existed, potential investors became interested in running Blockbuster. Cook, who went on to launch a number of other startups, sold his stores for a mere $18.5m to a waste management mogul, Wayne Huizenga, in 1987. Huizenga kept up the company's aggressive growth, opening stories across the United States and abroad.

During the time Hastings was building Pure Software, Blockbuster was slowly turning into an entertainment behemoth. It invested in music rentals and beat Japan's Nintendo in a lawsuit that allowed it to start renting video games. By 1994, a quick expansion had resulted in around 3,600 Blockbuster stores springing into existence and rival chains being purchased, including Ritz Video in the UK, and Huizenga was ready to move the business into new hands again. This time it reached a much higher price. US media group Viacom swooped in and splashed around $8.4bn on the video rental chain in a complex deal.

However, Viacom's takeover of Blockbuster turned into a messy affair. Three CEOs left between 1994 and 1997, before John Antioco, who would lead the firm for a decade, was installed in its top job. It was his role to revive the business, which by this time was faltering. Viacom took the company public in 1999 and raised $465m from selling 31 million shares at $15 each. The figure, given Blockbuster's previously high valuations as a multibillion-dollar company, can be considered measly but put it on a firmer footing to move into a second decade – a time when DVDs, online viewing and Netflix would emerge.

Despite popular opinion, Blockbuster wasn't averse to experimenting with technology. As early as 1999 it struck a deal with the internet provider AOL to provide content for its online offerings. It also attempted to get into on-demand online content with Enron in 2000 in a big way. The two companies announced a bold 20-year deal to sell movies to customers online, with the titles being delivered to PCs or TVs via the internet. People would use their internet connections with Enron to access movies from Blockbuster, once it had struck deals with studios giving it the rights to distribute video digitally. Ambitious targets forecast the service to be running by the end of the year and have up to 500 titles available to view.

Impressively, Enron managed to get the infrastructure needed in place and had small-scale consumer trials running a year after the partnership was agreed. Given online video-on-demand services didn't emerge properly until the middle of the decade, Blockbuster and Enron were well ahead of the competition.

Yet the project was doomed. In the middle of 2001,

just one year into the two-decade-long agreement, it was scrapped. Enron said Blockbuster was too slow in striking deals with Hollywood studios to license their films, and in return Blockbuster criticised the on-demand streaming technology, with the *Wall Street Journal* saying it had technical and security concerns.[9] A few months later Enron's accounting fraud, lies and shady dealings started to come to light and it filed for bankruptcy.

When Hastings and Randolph launched Netflix, they knew Blockbuster was its biggest competition even though the company didn't do home delivery or online rental. The sheer scale of its vast empire couldn't be ignored. With one decisive move, Blockbuster could knock the Netflix upstart out of existence.

Around the same time as Blockbuster was experimenting with video-on-demand, Hastings, Randolph and the chief financial officer, Barry McCarthy, flew to meet Blockbuster executives. Hastings took a bold proposal to the table: Netflix should take over Blockbuster's website and help it to rent DVDs. It has later been suggested that Hastings wanted $50m for 50 per cent of his company.

Recalling the proposed deal he said Blockbuster was courteous about the offer but it was probably the wrong thing to have done. 'If they had [accepted], we would have been 100 times bigger faster because we would have been blockbuster.com,' he said in a 2015 interview. 'We wanted to maintain control because we knew they would screw it up. In hindsight it was a little naive because it was too important for them to be able to say, "Okay we're going to give up the name and what that represents in exchange for half the equity." But it was worth a try.'[10]

Despite Blockbuster's efforts to continue to grow its physical stores towards the end of 2003, its leadership had realised an online DVD rental service would be necessary. In a 2011 *Harvard Business Review* article, Antioco explained why the firm was slow to move on digital: 'We weren't sure whether a model in which you managed your selections by means of a queue and got a movie in the mail a few days later would catch on.'[11] Netflix continued to pick up new subscribers and Blockbuster was falling behind. Despite having large debts, the company would only continue losing ground to Netflix in online DVD rental if it didn't have a hand in the game itself. There was also the added tension of Blockbuster's bricks-and-mortar high street stores and the worry that online rental would jeopardise them. But the time had come for Antioco to digitise.

In her book, *Netflixed: The Epic Battle for America's Eyeballs*, the journalist Gina Keating recounts the Blockbuster/Netflix battle in close detail. Blockbuster Online was launched in August 2004 – its purpose was to compete directly with Netflix. To do so it would offer an almost identical service priced at $19.99 per month, three dollars cheaper than its rival; which had raised its prices just months earlier.

At an elaborate launch event held at the Granada Theater in Dallas, Keating writes, Blockbuster demonstrated it was keen to outdo Hastings's upstart. Celebrity impersonators were hired to mingle with Blockbuster employees and guests. Ahead of the launch, a giant button had been added to the raised stage where Blockbuster executives were planning to push the service out to customers. The button was rigged to set Blockbuster Online live when it was pressed. And the direct taunts of Netflix started within seconds of the firm's presentation beginning.

Slides shown on a large screen flashed up quoting Hastings. The Blockbuster team picked one where he'd been deliberately taunting Blockbuster that it wouldn't be able to compete with Netflix and criticising its technology efforts and ability to promote its planned service. A different quotation flashed on screen: 'You have officially awakened a sleeping giant. Now let's go kick some ass.' Keating reports it was attributed to Antioco.

Senior Netflix staff were aghast when they first saw a trial of Blockbuster Online several months earlier, Keating says. The website was a carbon copy of the startup's and even included features such as the queue, where upcoming rental choices could be saved. It wasn't the last time that Blockbuster tried to directly copy the successes of Netflix.

Following the launch, Blockbuster executives decided it was time to ditch a huge part of its income by getting rid of late fees. However, the way it did so was slightly underhand. If its customers didn't return their rentals on time they'd be charged the buying price for the DVD or game they'd rented. If they then decided to return the title they'd be charged a fee, around $1.25, that was attributed to the cost of restocking. The plan backfired when regulators in 47 US states decided the fees weren't prominently advertised and as such were unfair on customers. The company agreed to pay $630,000 for the cost of their investigation and said it would change the way it advertised the fees.

As a price war between Blockbuster and Netflix progressed, Hastings took to publicly mocking his rival's efforts. 'Blockbuster is spending hundreds of millions of dollars, so when we beat them, it will be celebratory,' he said in an interview with *Inc* in 2005.[12] During an earnings call with investors in January of the same year, Hastings was asked about Blockbuster's impact on the company. 'In the last six months, Blockbuster has thrown everything but the kitchen sink at us,' he retorted.[13] This only prompted Antioco to send a kitchen sink addressed to Hastings to the Netflix offices.

Blockbuster's physical stores, run as franchises of the business, were a crucial part of its collapse. The locations were costly, and, as viewing habits changed, people started to spend more time using the internet to view media. Not just Netflix, but YouTube. After Blockbuster was spun out of Viacom in 2004 it had to restructure its debt three times to avoid bankruptcy, and faced lower revenues as time progressed.

But it wasn't just Blockbuster that Netflix faced early competition from. As well as rumours of an Amazon DVD rental service throughout Blockbuster's last decade, there was also Walmart. The retailer launched a semi-successful DVD rental business in 2002, and two years later was offering customers discs at a cheaper price than either Netflix or Blockbuster's initial $19.99 launch offering. Hastings managed to convince Walmart it was better suited to DVD sales than rentals by 2005. In the *Inc* interview Hastings said he had dinner with the CEO of Walmart.com and came to an agreement. Like its initial deal with Amazon, Netflix would push customers to Walmart's website for sales and in return it would tell them to rent from Netflix.

Also emerging was Redbox. The company, which still exists today, launched in 2002 as an offshoot of McDonald's. It consists of vending machines full of DVDs and video games that can be rented – originally they were designed as mini-shops and stocked everything from food to disposable cameras. After seeing more longevity in renting DVDs, the firm dropped other products and has expanded to thousands of locations across the US. Former Netflix executive Mitch Lowe worked at the company as chief operations officer and also its president. It allowed customers to return DVDs to any rental kiosk and charged as little as $1 per rental. While never seriously threatening to take on Blockbuster or Netflix the firm proved to be an unrelenting player in the DVD marketplace.

One of Blockbuster's final big pushes to combat Netflix's growth was Total Access. It launched in November 2006 and promised subscribers they could rent movies online and bring the DVDs back to any physical Blockbuster store when they were done with them; in addition, they would be able to pick up a new rental in store for free. Taking a DVD back to the store also automatically started the shipping process for the next title stored in the online queue.

Antioco hailed Total Access as a success, saying that by the end of 2006 the online rental arm of Blockbuster had 2.2 million subscribers – adding 500,000 of those in the third quarter when the scheme was launched. However, it was costly. Blockbuster struggled to make money from giving away free rentals. After a run-in with shareholders, Antioco left Blockbuster in 2007; his successor, James Keyes, was tasked with saving the business.

Barry Enderwick, who worked in the Netflix marketing team for 11 years, says in an interview that the company was able to predict Blockbuster's growth (or lack of it). Pulling together its opponent's subscriber numbers, growth rate and information the company proactively published, it built a tool to track Blockbuster's fortunes. During the entire competitive fight with the video incumbent, Enderwick says Hastings didn't appear to be rattled. 'He never panicked,' Enderwick says. 'He would just be like, "Here's what's actually happening, here's how we're going to attack it and here's why we think that's going to work." He would share all that information with the company.'

Before Antioco left he had one more run-in with Hastings. As when they had met just after the turn of the Millennium, there was a deal on the table. At the Sundance Film Festival in January 2007, Antioco told a *Bloomberg Game Changers* documentary some years later, Hastings flipped his earlier position and wanted to buy Blockbuster. In less than a decade, Netflix had gone from underdog to potentially swallowing its biggest rival whole. 'His preference would have been for Netflix to buy Blockbuster Online and what we proposed back was a merger,' the former Blockbuster CEO told Bloomberg.[14] However, the deal didn't go any further, as there were concerns about any merger being blocked under anti-trust rules; a combined version of Netflix and Blockbuster Online would have swamped the entire online rental market.

After departing Blockbuster, Antioco said he was sure Netflix had won. 'I sold my stock and bought a bunch of Netflix shares, which were then priced around $20,' he wrote in 2011, saying the decision wasn't an emotional investment. 'I could see that Netflix was going to have the whole DVD-by-mail market handed to it, along with a direct path to streaming movies into homes – which is exactly what Netflix has done.' He said he thought he was 'a genius' as he sold the shares a short time later when they reached $35 each – since then they've sky-rocketed.[15]

In Antioco's place at Blockbuster, Keyes, the former chief executive of the retailer 7-Eleven, inherited a company in a position of reasonable growth. During the first quarter of 2007 Blockbuster added 800,000 new subscribers to its online service (reaching a total of 2.8 million) and beat Netflix's growth for the period (it added 480,000 new members but it had 6.8 million subscribers overall). The promotion of Total Access was working and, combined with Blockbuster shutting some stores, helped it appear in a stronger position than previously. However, things were far from rosy.

After taking over Blockbuster's main role, Keyes set to transform the company into one that offered customers pretty much everything. In its desperation it struck a deal with Live Nation to start selling concert tickets at around 500 of the US stores it was keeping alive. At one stage

Blockbuster introduced the bizarre concept of allowing customers to download movies in-store. In the trials, conducted in Dallas, it let people bring their own portable devices into stores and put movies on them for $3.99 per time. (It didn't catch on.)

The thing that may have killed Blockbuster's hopes of defeating Netflix was a price change for its Total Access scheme. Although it was losing money when subscribers took advantage of free in-store rentals, the programme had helped to draw new online subscribers like never before. In January 2008 Keyes raised the Total Access price by $2–$10, depending on the subscription customers had. As well as raising prices, the large advertising budget for Total Access was decreased and the number of subscribers signing up for online DVD rental slowed. Blockbuster also attempted to pay $1bn for the electronics retailer Circuit City Stores to allow it to have a presence in a larger number of outlets that people would visit to buy other products. The deal didn't go through, though. And the company also started taking on Redbox's kiosk, giving the Blockbuster Express brand name to the vending machine company NCR Corp. The aim was to have 10,000 kiosks in place during 2010.

Keyes didn't follow Hastings into streaming – at least not in the same way as Netflix. It struck a number of deals with online video providers – including MovieLink – but the biggest was with Sonic Solutions, which would help it to provide 10,000 movies for rent and sale online. The titles would come from Blockbuster itself and CinemaNow, a firm purchased by Sonic. However, Blockbuster's online service wouldn't be subscription-based. Like iTunes and Amazon at the time, it would let people rent or download movies on a pay-per-view basis. If you wanted to watch a movie you would pay once to have access to it.

Keyes also took aim at Hastings's efforts. At one point in 2008 he dismissed Netflix, telling an investment website, *The Motley Fool*: 'Neither Redbox nor Netflix are even on the radar screen in terms of competition.'[16] In a separate interview with *PaidContent.org* he said he was 'confused by this fascination that everybody has with Netflix'. And in the same interview he claimed Netflix didn't 'really have or do anything that we can't or don't already do ourselves'.[17]

He told the *Los Angeles Times* in 2010 that Netflix was mostly useful for older shows; this was after Blockbuster had struck a deal with movie studios allowing it access to DVDs as soon as they were available[18] – although he did also praise Netflix in a *Fast Company* interview in 2010, saying Netflix had embraced the fact that it had a large amount of long-tail content and that its search engine was better than any others that existed.[19]

Blockbuster's ultimate downfall – it went into liquidation in late 2010 – was complicated and can't be attributed to a single factor. The growth of Netflix ultimately played a part in the video store's failure (as did other competitors, including Redbox), but it wasn't the only one. An aggressive takeover attempt by a shareholder, Carl Icahn, destabilised the company's management, a slow take-up of its online rental and streaming didn't help, it had high levels of debt from its days of being owned by Viacom, and, once the firm was competing, the underlying technology it produced couldn't keep up with Netflix.

During Antioco's tenure, Blockbuster had the best chance of defeating Netflix. It was able to pour huge amounts of money into the marketing of its service and to create a hype that Netflix didn't have the resources to do. 'Really, if they had started two years earlier they would have won, in perfect hindsight, because even though it was messy execution they would have overwhelmed us,' Hastings remarked in a 2014 talk at Stanford University's business school.[20]

Hastings has since said that some of his decisions were panicked. 'We got desperate and we did some dumb things,' he told the *New York Times* in 2013.[21] Netflix did experiment a lot during the years of its Blockbuster battle, trying to enhance its service to offer new products or features that could entice people in. For instance, Hastings said there were tests of online banner advertising around the titles on its site, the launch of its own studio division, Red Envelope Entertainment, and its purchase of new, untested titles from the Sundance Film Festival.

'After we eventually won the Blockbuster battle, I looked back and realised all those things distracted us. They didn't help, and they marginally hurt,' he told the publication. 'The reason we won is because we improved our everyday service of shipping and delivering. That experience grounded us. Executing better on the core mission is the way to win.'

4

A CULTURE OF FREEDOM

Sometime in 1997, Patty McCord was woken in the middle of the night by a phone call. Reed Hastings was on the other end of the line and he wanted to talk. He was starting a new company that was going to be the Amazon of DVD rentals and he wanted her to join the team.

McCord, who described the fateful call in her book, *Powerful*, had worked with Hastings at Pure Software, joining in 1994 and running the firm's human resources (HR) division. She had been a driving force in helping Pure to hire the right people, and everything was done by the book.

But with this new company called Netflix, Hastings said, things would be different. The business wouldn't be run in the same way as others. This time they would create a new internal culture and make the place somewhere people enjoyed working. McCord agreed. She spent the next 14 years at the business, driving the corporate culture.

Netflix has a radical business culture and a large part of this comes from Hastings. Netflix believes in honesty and freedom for staff members to take decisions and make mistakes. If staff members don't stick to the principles that are set out then they are fired. This means staff who work for Hastings can be incredibly loyal, or if they don't like the company's culture, they can leave pretty soon after being hired.

Hastings's approach to how the company should be run became evident in 2009, when he decided to publish its internal staff document. Known as the Netflix Culture Deck, it's a 125-page series of slides that covers the staff work ethic, their responsibilities, how the company hires people, what they will be paid and details concerning firings too.[1] The document was first created by Hastings, McCord and other Netflix executives.

Making the culture deck available online was a smart move. It was being sent to all the people who were interviewing for jobs at Netflix, and Hastings argues that if he had not published it then eventually someone applying for a job would have leaked it.

But beyond trying to stop reputational damage, it has proved popular. 'It may well be the most important document ever to come out of the Valley,' Facebook's chief operating officer, Sheryl Sandberg, told GQ magazine in 2013.[2] There have been more than 18 million views of the document on the file-sharing website Slideshare. It has also acted as a great advertisement for what it is like to work at Netflix. Potential staff members who don't like its cut-throat nature wouldn't have to wait until the interview stage to find out it wasn't for them. And, conversely, clearly stating what employees will and won't get is an important recruitment tool that can attract the people Hastings wants.

It has changed over time and has been adapted as the company has grown. Hastings and staff continue to work on Netflix's culture, and he's repeatedly said the company's attitudes change each year.

Netflix's original culture deck is bullet-point heavy. Most of the slides don't feature too many words and they're often focused on some key ideas. (Some of these will be explored further in this chapter and later in chapter 7.)

There are seven key areas to Netflix's culture: values, high performance, freedom and responsibility, context, high alignment, high pay and employee development.

The document says businesses shouldn't focus on values that exist for face-value purposes, or they will end up like the corrupt failure that was Enron, and that Netflix only wants to hire the best people for the jobs it has. Netflix makes it clear that it isn't all about flashy perks – such as giant parties and huge bonuses being given out every year. 'An employee who doesn't work out usually knows it and the parting is mutual,' Hastings said in an interview with *Business Insider* in 2011. 'We hire a lot of seasoned people but we don't have all the perks – cubes, not offices; very few assistants; small staffs; no traditional HR support (plan your own offsite!).'[3]

Instead, Hastings defines it as a place where people go to

work, enjoy what they do and are successful. 'Some find that refreshing, others learn quickly that they're accustomed to all the trappings and aren't comfortable without them,' he said. While Netflix may not offer the corporate rewards in the same way that other businesses do, it will pay staff as much as it can and give them the space that they need to flourish into better people and workers. If people don't perform to the standards expected, then they will be let go with a 'generous' severance package.

In a phone call, McCord recalls Hastings's attitude to how Netflix should be run was akin to that of an engineer. She says: 'He approached culture like he approached product, which is: "What's the problem you are solving? And is this the best way to do it?"'

'What I learnt from him was, everything that I took for granted he would say, "Why do we do this?", and out of my mouth would come the typical: "It's against the law" or "Everybody else does it that way",' she says. Hastings would question everything. 'And he was just intolerant of either one of those answers.

'If I said it was against the law, he wanted to see the law. And then I realised I didn't really know some of those things were illegal.' McCord adds that if it was suggested the company should do things in a way that was considered best practice within the human resources industry, Hastings would want to know who thought it was a best practice, how the company knew that it actually worked and whether there were data or measurements to back up the approach.

She says it was how you would run a company if you were starting without an idea of how other businesses did things. 'If you could start with a blank sheet of paper, would this be the best way? And I think that's my most enduring lesson from working with him.'

While the culture deck could be seen as Silicon Valley idealism, former staff members say it is preached within the company. 'I think of the culture deck as sort of, like the American Constitution, it is an attempt to self-prescribe what Netflix is and what we aspire to be,' John Ciancutti, a former Netflix vice-president, says in a phone call. While he was at the company, VPs would go away for a week of the year together to discuss business priorities. A large part of this time would be talking about the culture deck.

People do get freedom and are trusted to experiment with the work they're doing. There is an honesty across the company, with staff members being able to challenge the ideas of others and come up with alternative solutions to the problems they're working on.

In recent years, the slide deck has been replaced by a slightly newer document detailing Netflix's culture that lives on its jobs website. The culture webpage is largely the same as the slideshow (although formatted in a more user-friendly way).[4] The same values and principles are outlined, although there is one newer section.

Inclusion is expanded in Netflix's current culture document. Staff are required to 'nurture and embrace' different perspectives; they must realise they hold biases and work to overcome them, intervene if someone is being marginalised and be curious about how different backgrounds affect people at work.

Having an open culture doesn't mean it is a free-for-all. There are – obviously – rules. The original culture deck said there were two broad types of necessary restrictions. First, preventing any irrevocable disaster (getting financial statements wrong; hackers stealing customer information), and, second, moral, ethical and legal issues. The newer culture document shows that Netflix has grown up and moved out of its startup days. It says zero-tolerance issues include the harassment of employees, trading on insider information and similar issues that would in most cases be illegal. It also says that there are strict controls and rules concerning who can access the payment information of its subscribers and there are limits on the amount of cash that can be transferred from company bank accounts. These are all largely sensible policies for a company to have, but where Netflix is really different is in the policies it doesn't have.

Hastings has said for the first few years the company was running, 'all we cared about was survival'. In a 2015 talk hosted by the venture capital firm Kleiner Perkins Caufield & Byers, he said everyone's focus was on whether its business model would work and if people actually wanted to rent DVDs online.[5]

After its IPO in 2002 the company started to take its culture and staff practices more seriously. It's the point when the culture deck first started to be written. 'Now that we're public and we're going to be around for a while we should be more articulate with new employees,' Hastings said of his attitude at the time. Initially the slides were used as an employee orientation document that was intended to help introduce them to the company. Hastings said when hiring staff, managers often told potential employees about Netflix's culture and its non-traditional approaches. But people who hadn't been told about how the company operated were in for a big surprise. He said: 'The people [for] who this was the first time they'd seen it would fall off of their chairs.'

Team players only

Working at Netflix is like being part of a sports team, Hastings says. Within the company everyone has their role, responsibilities and duties, and it's up to each member of staff to fulfil all of them. Like the manager of a competitive sports team he wants the best people to be in each position that is available. The metaphor is clichéd but it appears to work for Netflix's purposes.

Adrian Cockcroft, who spent six years in Netflix's engineering teams, including as a director of web engineering, says that from his experience the sports team analogy is practised within the business. When he joined the company in 2007, it was just transitioning to streaming and this was considered a coming of age.

'The sports team was growing up through minor leagues or a high-school level team, through to being one of the best teams in the top leagues,' Cockcroft explains in a phone call. 'And that was the way we talked about it internally. So as we grew the company, every now and again somebody that had been there quite a long time would get pushed out.'

For people who make the team, Netflix pays very well. Hastings's attitude is to pay at the top of the market rate for people. The company is known for paying salaries that easily match the likes of those from Google, Amazon and Facebook. This means in the highly competitive world of Silicon Valley the company is able to fight for the best engineers and technical experts.

His idea is that one employee who excels at their job and gets more done will get paid a high amount but overall they'll cost less than two staff members are who are only adequate. (Netflix says it won't downgrade people's pay if the company goes through hard times.) Staff salaries are re-evaluated each year based on the market value for those employees. The result is that there isn't a regular percentage pay rise that's set for each individual or one that applies across the entire business.

Netflix filings to the US Securities and Exchange Commission showed that Hastings and chief content officer Ted Sarandos would both get a combined salary and set of stock options worth $31.5m during 2019. As the company's content business has grown – picking up a host of industry awards – Sarandos's success has seen him reach the same levels of pay as the CEO. (Netflix scrapped performance bonuses in 2018 after US laws were changed.) Unlike some other companies, employees get to decide how much of their salary they receive in stock options. If a person wanted to, they could take an entire year's worth of pay in stock, or take no Netflix stock at all and receive their entire salary in cash.

But big salaries come with a cost: high performance is expected. 'Sustained A-level performance, despite minimal effort, is rewarded with more responsibility and great pay,' the original Netflix culture deck says. People who put in a lot of effort and don't get good results aren't wanted at the company. 'The worst thing is for a manager to come in and tell me: "Let's give Susie a huge raise because she's always in the office,"' Hastings said in 2007. 'What do I care? I want managers to come to me and say: "Let's give a really big raise to Sally because she's getting a lot done" – not because she's chained to her desk.'[6]

Hastings, and Netflix's culture document, outline that within a sports team only the best players will get picked to represent a club. 'It is up to the coach to ensure that every player on the field is amazing at their position, and plays very effectively with the others,' the company says about its culture. It defines a good team member as being someone who is trying to achieve a common goal (having Netflix be streaming everywhere and make money), cares about the other people in their team and wants to work with people who are extraordinary at their jobs.

For the people who do get employed by Netflix there may be the high salaries but there isn't a focus on perks. 'Our version of the great workplace is not sushi lunches, great gyms, fancy offices, or frequent parties,' Netflix's current company culture document says. That doesn't mean it doesn't do these things to some extent – it's just not stated as one of its priorities. The company's offices in Los Angeles and Los Gatos have free food for employees on most floors, are airy and spacious, plus feature plenty of meeting rooms and breakout spaces for staff to work away from their desks.

Hastings's team approach is the opposite of many companies: the idea of it being a family is one that doesn't apply. Business leaders and CEOs – particularly when a company is struggling – tend to rely on describing their companies as tightly knit units. They stick together, are loyal to each other, and won't abandon people who are behaving badly.

For Hastings, that approach doesn't work. 'Yes, we have deep relationships, yes, we care about each other, but ultimately you've got a certain number of players on the field and you need extraordinary performance in every position to achieve the team's goals,' he said to an audience of the Utah Technology Council in 2018.[7] 'Unlimited loyalty to a shrinking firm, or to an ineffective employee, is not what we are about,' the culture deck says.

This way of running a company is ruthless but the team metaphor is useful for helping Netflix to justify its hard decisions. Acting like a team, Hastings has said, allows Netflix to hire only the best people it can, develop those who already work at the company and cut people when it needs too.

For people who don't live up to expectations there's one

clear message: 'Adequate performance gets a generous severance package.' Using the sports team analogy this makes sense: if a leading goal or points scorer stops getting results they'll be dropped from the team and eventually sold. Judging people on their performance makes firing staff easier. 'It doesn't feel like heresy, it doesn't feel awful, because you set up the model that it's like professional sports,' Hastings said in Utah.

Managers inside Netflix are encouraged to decide whether they should continue employing staff using one method: the keeper test. The culture deck describes it thus: 'Which of my people, if they told me they were leaving, for a similar job at a peer company, would I fight hard to keep at Netflix?' If a manager feels unsure about a person or couldn't justify why it's crucial for them to be doing their role, they can let them go. Equally, it is the responsibility of managers to make sure their staff are given context about the work they're trying to complete. They're told to make sure people know why they're doing a certain task and how it feeds into the company's wider aims.

Hastings offers employees who are let go an average severance package of four months' pay. (He's previously said that if it's realised in the first two weeks that there's been a genuine hiring mistake – not a breach of contract – even then the person will get fourth months' pay when they are let go.) The high figure makes it easier for managers to get rid of people without feeling guilty about doing so. It gives the employee some financial security while looking for a new job once they've left Netflix. McCord has said it wasn't uncommon during her 14 years at Netflix for senior staff to help find new jobs for the people who were leaving the company.

Netflix isn't completely cut-throat in firing people, though. If someone who performed well in their role starts to struggle, the culture document says they 'get a near term pass' because it's possible that they'll start doing excellent work again in the future.

Hastings also encourages his employees to be looking around for other jobs – not because he wants to lose staff members, but because he says they should have an idea of what they're worth and what the competition can offer. The culture deck says: 'It's a healthy idea, not a traitorous one, to understand what other firms would pay you, by interviewing and talking to peers at other companies.'

A ruthless approach

While Netflix's culture may be distinct, it certainly isn't for everyone. This is partly why the company offers high severance packages for the people who don't make the grade. Many people working for Hastings seem to be incredibly loyal and often stay within the company for lengthy periods of time. Others have quickly moved on and left the business. (Research into former employees revealed that many now work in senior positions at direct-streaming competitors and other giant tech firms: Facebook, Apple, Amazon, YouTube and Google all feature heavily.)

One report from the *Wall Street Journal* in 2018 revealed

how Netflix's open and honest culture can lead to firings and a level of public scrutiny that not everyone will be comfortable with.[8] The newspaper, speaking to 70 current and former Netflix staff, said each person at director level can see the salaries of every employee. Staff can be fearful for their positions as they're aware people who don't perform well are removed from their roles.

Once a person has been fired, it is not uncommon for emails to be sent around large groups of people explaining why they no longer work there. A former vice-president at the company, Sean Carey, told the newspaper he attended a meeting about why he had been fired in front of around 40 other employees. 'It was certainly awkward for some, but was also consistent with the culture – there is sometimes a cost to transparency,' Carey said, adding he thought the process was beneficial for him.

Nobody is immune from firing or the keeper test. The *Wall Street Journal* reported that the chief product officer, Neil Hunt, was fired by Hastings as the business had moved on and one of his staff, Greg Peters, was the best person for the job.

In December 2012, McCord left the business. She has never publicly revealed the circumstances surrounding her departure but she was let go. 'Eventually, when we worked together at Netflix, Reed and I both had to come to terms with the fact that it was time for me to go,' she wrote in her book, *Powerful*, adding: 'I had tremendous respect for Reed's discipline to choose his team for the future.'[9] (McCord now preaches Netflix's culture to other companies and works with startups to develop their own practices.)

Former members of staff say one of Hastings's biggest weaknesses is an occasional disconnect from others around him. 'He says exactly what he thinks, he's not worried about social niceties,' explains John Ciancutti, who worked at Netflix for 12 years. In a phone call he says Hastings is 'very willing' to admit when things are his fault and when he has failed. This applies to staff as well. 'What you're doing is very hard, and you're going to make mistakes, you're going to fail.' Ciancutti says failure is a resource that is used for learning.

'There's not a lot of sentiment around Reed: [he's] very logical, very friendly, very easy, approachable, very honest, but he's not emotional in the way he does things,' Adrian Cockcroft, a former engineering member of staff, says. 'Occasionally when he's got things wrong, it's because he's underestimated the reactions other people would have.'

'He was a tough boss, you know, he didn't shy away from criticism or letting you know if he thought you didn't do a great job,' adds Mitch Lowe, who was a vice-president of business development at the company. However, he praises Hastings for getting the most out of his staff by giving them the freedom to do their best work.

Other senior executives who have left in recent years have done so in difficult circumstances. Hastings's head of public relations, Jonathan Friedland, who was with the company for six years, is said to have used the N-word twice during meetings with staff. ('Leaders have to be beyond reproach in the example we set and unfortunately I fell short of that standard when I was insensitive in speaking to my team about words that offend in comedy,' he tweeted publicly after he was fired. 'I feel awful about the distress this lapse caused to people at a company I love and where I want everyone to feel included and appreciated.'[10]) Friedland was later replaced by Rachel Whetstone, a veteran of Facebook and Uber's PR teams.

Hastings handled the firing with an honest email to staff, which was reported on and published in full by the *Hollywood Reporter*.[11] The email shows the company's levels of openness. Hastings described two occasions when Friedland used the word and said he had failed to bring the incident up when speaking to the company's black employee group.

'As I reflect on this, at this first incident, I should have done more to use it as a learning moment for everyone at Netflix about how painful and ugly that word is, and that it should not be used,' Hastings wrote. 'I realize that my privilege has made me intellectualize or otherwise minimize race issues like this. I need to set a better example by learning and listening more so I can be the leader we need.'

He then detailed some of the complexities of the racial word and said the company would look at more ways to 'educate and help our employees broadly understand the many difficult ways that race, nationality, gender identity and privilege play out in society and our organization'.

The email was signed off thanking Friedland for his work at the company over the years but saying 'his lack of judgment in this area was too big for him to remain'. Hastings then said details of the firing would appear in the press pretty soon after the email was sent.

According to the *Wall Street Journal*, when Hastings had found out that Friedland's firing had been leaked to the press, he sent an email to senior staff. He said that whoever had spread the news outside the company should tell human resources about it. He wrote: 'You'll get a discreet quiet exit, and our generous severance package if you do it now.' Hastings later apologised. The paper reported that he sent another note to staff saying: 'crazy stuff happens in the fog of war'.

5

INTERNET TV IS BORN

As Reed Hastings launched Netflix in 1997, the World Wide Web was unrecognisable compared to the beast it is today. To get online, DSL cables had to be plugged into glitchy modems, dialling tones allowed people to get online, and AOL was a primary tool in doing so. The year before, *Time* magazine had published a list of the 'top websites' for 1996:[1] the Library of Congress was ranked alongside a growing book retailer called Amazon, and the list even included one site called *The Kevin Bacon Game*, which tried to prove a theory that every actor in Hollywood had been in a movie with Bacon or someone who had co-starred with him.

At this point, the internet wasn't ready for streaming video (or even efficient downloads of large files). This didn't stop Hastings and his staff from trying to create ways for people to access video from Netflix over the internet.

Originally, Hastings thought video downloads would be the way Netflix reached people through the internet, and there were two early internal tests of this.

The first attempt in 2000 created a way for people to download movies. The project faced one big challenge: it took 16 hours for a film to be ready to watch because broadband was in its infancy – it cost $10 in fees for the internet traffic. As *Fortune* reported in 2010, Hastings shut the project down.[2] There was another attempt at downloads in 2003 as staff created a $300 Netflix box, which had its own hard drive that stored movies but would take six hours to download them – a slight improvement but not one that would be good enough for customers.

A decade after Netflix was launched, internet speeds and connectivity began to improve, which coincided with the formation of some of the web's biggest tech giants, but streaming full movies in high definition still wasn't realistic. Yet in January 2007 Hastings decided the time was right to start letting people watch Netflix through their PCs. Two years earlier YouTube had launched and shown internet pioneers that video over the web didn't have to be downloaded; it could be watched whenever the viewer wanted.

Hastings created a system called 'Instant Watch'. At no extra charge, subscribers could have shows streamed over the internet by simply selecting them from Netflix's website. These would play without downloading the entire movie or episode; titles that could be streamed had a 'play' button appear next to Netflix's traditional 'add to queue' option. Just a few months later Netflix would deliver its one billionth DVD: a copy of the drama *Babel* was sent from a distribution centre in Houston to a home in Helotes, Texas.

At its launch the streaming service was incredibly limited and mainstream adoption would take 'a number of years'. Around 1,000 titles could be streamed to begin with and Netflix wanted to seriously increase this figure. The streaming offering was contrasted with its DVD business, which had more than 70,000 titles and tried to give subscribers a choice of everything that was available. Movie and TV studios were largely supportive and Netflix signed up some titles from NBC Universal, Sony, MGM, 20th Century Fox, Paramount and Warner Brothers.

When Netflix began streaming, it was only possible to watch movies and shows through a computer – watching on TVs would come later. To be able to stream, the PC had to be a recent Windows computer with the Internet Explorer browser. The Netflix subscriber had to download a special piece of software to let them play shows. And a robust internet connection was needed: one Mbps (megabit per second) would let streaming work, while a three Mbps connection allowed DVD-quality pictures to be watched.

The idea of binge-watching Netflix didn't come with the introduction of streaming. There were limits in place to begin with. When it was first launched, the amount of TV people could watch over the internet was based upon their existing subscription plan. If you paid for the $5.99 DVD plan then you could watch six hours of streamed video; the

$17.99 plan allowed 18 hours of streaming. If a subscriber started watching a movie, got six minutes in and decided they didn't want to watch it, they'd only lose the actual amount of time viewed.

Six months after streaming was launched, Netflix had doubled the number of viewing options to 2,000 and said it would hit 5,000 by the end of 2007. During its initial months the company bragged that the Instant Watch feature had been used five million times, with *The Office* and *The Matrix* being among the most-watched content.

But Hastings knew that streaming needed to be available on more than just PCs. Without expanding the amount of devices that Netflix could be streamed to it would be impossible to keep growing the number of subscribers. As streaming started, Hastings was already envisioning getting on to more devices. 'We'll work to get to every internet-connected screen,' he said in an announcement, citing not only TVs but mobile phones as well. The target market was also clear. Hastings predicted that people under 30 would be more likely to sign up to streaming, while those who were older, 'maybe they won't get into it'.[3]

One year after its launch, the number of streaming titles had hit 6,000, and, more importantly, deals were starting to be struck with hardware manufacturers. One of the first was LG, whose high-definition TVs would have the technical ability to connect to Netflix and stream shows, bypassing the need for a computer and greatly improving the watching experience for people who wanted to stream. At the same time, Netflix allowed people subscribing to its unlimited DVD plans an unlimited amount of streaming as well. The $1 per hour of streaming cost was dropped for its seven million subscribers.

A huge coup for Hastings was getting the manufacturers of games consoles to buy into the idea of streaming Netflix. The first to bite was Microsoft. Netflix was introduced to the Xbox 360 in November 2008 and fed into Microsoft's plan for its console to be a key entertainment feature, beyond gaming, in its customers' living rooms. The integration was an instant hit for both companies: within the first three months more than 1.5 billion minutes of movies and TV shows had been watched and more than one million Xbox owners had downloaded the Netflix app on to their consoles. By 2010, Netflix was also available on Sony's PlayStation and the Nintendo Wii.

Some early customers and reviewers complained that the Netflix streaming service on their consoles didn't have a huge choice of movies to watch. The user interface was initially very basic, with just a single row of shows being shown. But, for Hastings, the strategy was to get on to all the big consoles as quickly as possible, get people signed up to Netflix, and then make the viewing experience better as time went on. The consistent challenge would be getting enough shows that people wanted to see.

During Netflix's early DVD days it benefited from a piece of US law that allowed it to buy and distribute discs. The 'first sale doctrine' is a copyright law that lets the buyer of copyrighted work sell it on without having to pay any further fees to the copyright holder.

For Hastings this meant Netflix could buy DVDs from anywhere and rent them. The law really does mean anywhere – Netflix's chief content officer, Ted Sarandos, has said that in the early days the company would buy DVDs from Walmart and Best Buy if they couldn't get copies through the studios. This allowed the company to quickly build up its inventory and offer more choice.

However, when it came to streaming, Hastings didn't have the same protections. The first-sale doctrine doesn't apply. To be able to share movies and TV shows, Netflix has to buy the rights from the studios that hold the licences to them. As Netflix pushed into streaming this posed a problem: people wanted to watch huge, well-known shows and movies, and it would have to pay more to license them. While Netflix's recommendation algorithm could help to show people new films and TV shows they might enjoy, it couldn't totally replace the need for blockbusters.

Hastings found a clever way around this. As well as striking streaming deals with the big Hollywood studios, the company also went into partnership with Starz – a company with 16 subscriber-only movie channels. In a loophole as beneficial as the first doctrine, the contracts allowed Starz to sell Netflix its rights to stream movies online.

At the start of October 2008, around a year after Netflix started streaming, the Starz deal was announced. (The company had abandoned its own movie-downloading service, Vongo, a few months before.) As a result around 2,500 movies from Starz were added to Netflix. But it wasn't the quantity that mattered – the quality of the films was crucial for Netflix. Included in the titles were *Spider-Man 3*, *Pirates of the Caribbean*, *Superbad*, *No Country for Old Men* and other contemporary titles from Disney and Sony that would be an incentive for people to subscribe to Netflix.

The deal would last for three and a half years and, in what proved to be a bargain, Netflix is reported to have paid Starz $30m per year to stream its shows. When the deal was struck it was a huge sum for Netflix, which had eight million subscribers and only streamed to PCs. (Over the course of the deal it ran into some problems. In 2009 Sony demanded it remove some of its movies from the service as Netflix streaming them via Starz violated some of its contractual agreements.)

'When we did the Starz deal in 2008, we almost walked away from it because it was so much money for an activity that basically didn't happen, i.e. streaming, at the time,' Hastings told *Business Insider* in 2011.[4] Hastings was speaking months before the Starz deal was set to end and said he expected to pay a lot more to renew it that time around.

Across the duration of the Starz deal a huge amount changed for Netflix. Streaming had taken off, the company had struck deals with the major console and TV manufacturers, and growth had swelled. Even with the loss of 800,000 subscribers from the Qwikster problem (see later in this chapter for more), Netflix still had 23.8 million subscribers, almost treble the number it had when it originally agreed to pay to stream the high-end movies. As a result, the *Los Angeles Times* reported, executives at Starz told Hastings his firm would have to pay $300m per year to get the deal renewed. Ultimately the two companies couldn't come to an agreement.[5]

In September 2011, Starz publicly announced that its movies would be removed from Netflix at the start of the next year. Huge films such as *Toy Story 3*, *Tron* and *Tangled* were stripped from Netflix, which tried to downplay the importance of the loss by saying that Starz films had accounted for 8 per cent of its viewing, but because of its efforts to get films and TV shows from elsewhere this figure had dropped to just 2 per cent.

Emulating Apple

Hastings had a fascination with hardware. During his time at Stanford University, he invented his first product. The computer science course he was studying, which involved intense spells of coding, gave Hastings the idea to reinvent the computer mouse. He thought the solution to repetitive clicking and moving the cursor around, which meant the computer user had to take their hands away from the keyboard every few minutes, was to create a foot mouse. The device, he recounted in talks on entrepreneurship in 2015 and 2016, sat under a desk and let the user click by standing on a button.

He worked on creating it with a mechanical-engineering student and thought the device would help coders move between windows at lightning speed. 'I was so excited about patenting this device, I was going to be the foot mouse company,' he said. 'All my friends were sick of me because all I would do is touch their feet and try to feel how they were on the foot mouse.'

Things, however, weren't meant to be. 'It turns out if you do this for more than a few minutes your foot gets really sore and the mouse gets really dirty,' Hastings said. 'The thing I thought would be transformative in human productivity turned out to be a disaster.'

Netflix's own attempt with hardware wasn't quite a disaster but it was costly. Under the code name Project Griffin, Hastings decided that if the company developed a set-top box users could connect to the internet and the TV, they would be able to stream or download shows in the comfort of their living rooms, rather than on their PCs. So work began on the project.

The company sank resources into creating the software and hardware needed for the device. The result was a plain black box, with a Netflix logo on the front right corner, of a similar shape and size to a large box of chocolates. A report in 2013 by *Fast Company*, the US business magazine, said Netflix staff were excited about the streaming-box project – around 20 had been working on it – which its teams had put a huge amount of work into.

Netflix staff created an internal video, obtained by *Fast Company*, which documented the creation of Project Griffin. The footage was a spoof of the TV show *Lost*'s secretive organisation, the Dharma Initiative. (Netflix staff can be seen wearing giant lab coats, and the footage flickers in a way that suggests it is an old tape that has been lost for many years and has just been rediscovered.)

The video shows Netflix staff travelling to the Chinese offices of Foxconn, which creates electronics components on a contractual basis for other companies. It shows employees taking naps during breaks with their heads on their workstations. Cut back to Netflix offices and one member of the Griffin team shows Hastings the best way to sleep at the desk he's sitting at.

However, the player never made it to production. Overnight, Hastings decided he didn't want to release the hardware to the public. The cancellation was swift and came as a shock to staff who had been working on the device. The former chief financial officer, Barry McCarthy, who went on to work for the music-streaming company Spotify, told the *Wall Street Journal* not long after the streaming player was axed that he'd had reservations about moving into hardware. 'We don't even know what we don't know about this business,' he recalled thinking at the time. When the publication asked about Hastings's enthusiasm for creating hardware, he called it 'Apple lust'.

In the same article, Hastings said he had wanted to emulate Steve Jobs. 'Every entrepreneur is a Steve Jobs wannabe,' he says. 'I was as guilty of that as anybody.' Similarly, *Fast Company*'s report on the streaming device quoted an anonymous Netflix executive recalling a conversation with Hastings where they allege he was worried that Jobs wouldn't answer his phone calls about putting Netflix on the Apple TV streaming service if he saw Hastings as a hardware competitor. Hastings appeared on stage alongside Jobs in 2010 when Apple revealed the iPhone 4. He was there to unveil the first Netflix app for Apple's phone, which allowed mobile viewing for the first time. Netflix was also one of the initial apps available for the iPad when it was launched that year.

Ultimately, the work on the streaming box wasn't wasted. Hastings spun the hardware project out into the company Roku. On 20 May 2008 Roku announced its first streaming box, the DVP, and in the ensuing decade has released seven generations of products, which now take the shape of USB-stick-sized devices that plug into TVs or laptops. One review of the initial box, which was designed to be the Netflix box but had the company logo replaced with Roku's, said it was quiet, and cheap at $99, but that the streaming quality wasn't particularly good.

Netflix may not have produced any of its own devices except for this ill-fated box, but hardware has been present in Hastings's Netflix strategy since the company's earliest days. To help growth for the fledgling disc-rental business, the company struck deals with the creators of DVD players to have free-trial vouchers put within the packaging.

Since moving away from DVDs, Netflix has also agreed a series of lucrative deals with TV manufacturers, allowing for Netflix buttons to be added to remotes that instantly launch the streaming platform when pressed. Deals were made with big games console manufacturers – Sony, Microsoft and Nintendo – to support the Netflix apps and their gaming stores. The company also has a recommended TV scheme in which it suggests the best tech for people to buy to watch its shows and regularly works with the creators of TVs on unreleased models to work out the best ways to display its shows.

At Netflix's Los Gatos, California, headquarters there's a whole room dedicated to testing Netflix on mobile phones, iPads and other tablets. Hundreds of devices, from brand-new handsets to relatively old models, sit inside a cooled server room and run different versions of the Netflix app. The teams use the hardware to find bugs within its code that could cause an app to crash while it's being used.

The growth of Netflix after 2007 was fuelled by streaming, and the success it had can be attributed to its hardware strategy. Getting Netflix on all the major consoles and then into TVs helped people to easily sign up to its streaming service. It also gave people additional incentives to buy consoles: the box costing several hundred dollars wouldn't just sit in the corner and be used for gaming – it could also be a source of television entertainment.

His biggest mistake

Towards the end of September 2011, Hastings sat outside Netflix's Los Gatos offices in front of a camera. The setting was casual: he was on a patio and in the background were metallic tables and chairs, two similarly styled rubbish bins, a patch of grass and a giant waist-height plant pot.

Wearing an informal teal shirt, with at least three buttons undone, and a dark-blue V-neck T-shirt underneath, he sat alongside Andy Rendich, a Netflix staffer who had joined in 2003. On the table in front of Hastings was his laptop, with a pair of sunglasses lazily perched on top and a trademark Netflix red DVD delivery envelope. The sunny setup, which also featured part of a car park and the beige walls of nearby buildings, would have been well suited to the pair taking a relaxed outdoor break or enjoying a drink at the end of the day.

Instead Hastings was there to issue an apology for a decision he had made just three months earlier. In July 2011 he hiked the prices of members' subscriptions. The price change was extreme. In a press release announcing the changes Netflix bragged that its new DVD rental plan, which allowed customers to have one disc out at a time but an unlimited number across a month, was the 'lowest price ever'. The subscription cost just $7.99 per month, the same price as its unlimited streaming deal and was an aggressive move.

Beyond the bravado of the news was the fact that the combined unlimited DVD and streaming plan was being scrapped. Now, to get both, subscribers would have to fork out $15.98 per month – a 60 per cent increase on the previous $9.99 that was in place. The increase was introduced as Netflix's leadership realised a $10 plan for DVDs and streaming wouldn't adequately cover the costs of mailing out multiple discs a month to customers. The demand for DVDs was still high, but at the point of the price rise the burgeoning streaming option had only existed for four years and helped to push the overall subscriber count up to 20 million.

'We're making this video today to apologise in person, or at least on camera, for something that we did recently,' Hastings said.[6] He appeared relaxed as he spoke to the camera in the makeshift outdoor studio. The price rise had caused outrage with customers and many were not renewing their subscriptions. Over the course of the three-minute video he talked up the benefits of streaming – 'streaming is instant, streaming is fairly global' – and forecast, rightly, that in the years ahead DVDs would be dwarfed by shows sent to devices over the internet.

But instead of apologising for the price increase Hastings said sorry for something completely different. The way he handled the change was wrong, he said. 'I didn't make the communication and we didn't explain why we were doing it.' The argument was that if subscribers had been properly told about the separation they would have accepted it.

In fact, Hastings doubled down on the business decision to divide DVDs and streaming. The price would stay the same and Rendich, who had been sitting silently watching his boss talking, would become the CEO of a new Netflix spinoff: Qwikster, a name that referred to quick delivery times. Netflix.com would stay as Netflix.com and be the home of its streaming operations.

At the same time as Rendich, who had a background running Netflix's DVD operations, and Hastings released the video, the CEO also wrote an email to customers. The message was much the same: we made a mistake by not telling you about the price increase. 'In hindsight, I slid into arrogance based upon past success,' Hastings wrote. 'We have done very well for a long time by steadily improving our service, without doing much CEO communication.'[7]

Qwikster.com, which failed quickly, was doomed from the start. The underlying assumption that streaming movies and TV series would eventually be wildly more popular than physical discs was correct, but the time was not right to cast the hardware into its own division. DVDs were still popular with the Netflix subscriber base, who felt an affinity with receiving deliveries of red envelopes. (Hastings has said he underestimated the 'depth of emotional attachment' people had towards his company.)

The way Qwikster was set up didn't help either. Making people visit a separate website to order DVDs wasn't an ideal customer experience; neither was making ratings of films and queues of requested movies non-transferable. A planned logo change on the DVD envelopes will also have been a small, but ultimately significant, annoyance as well.

Hastings and Rendich went out of their way to say that while Netflix streaming and Qwikster DVD rental would be on different websites, they were trying to keep the same feel across both platforms. One big change was planned for Qwikster, though. For the first time, despite rumours in the very early days of the company, it would start to rent video games. Owners of Microsoft's Xbox 360, Sony's PlayStation 3 and Nintendo's Wii would be able to pay a small extra charge to rent and play the latest titles. If successful, the move would have provided a sweetener for those who were still wedded to renting the physical format.

The enterprise was rushed and a reaction to the impact of the huge price change that upset subscribers. In the weeks before the service was due to launch properly, Netflix didn't even own the @qwikster Twitter handle. The account was registered in the name of Jason Castillo and featured a picture of the *Muppet Show* character Fozzie Bear smoking cannabis. After the Qwikster brand name was revealed, Castillo tweeted that other users on the social network had inquired how much he'd be willing to sell the @ handle for.[8]

During the planning process, Hastings was warned that Qwikster didn't appear to be a step in the right direction. He told the *New York Times* that when explaining the plan to a friend, while soaking in a hot tub, they had reacted by saying it was an 'awful' idea.[9] At some level, staff at Netflix must have known this. Hastings's apology letter which was released with the video even said that once people had seen the footage they'd 'probably say we should avoid going into movie making'.

On 11 October 2011, a quick line was drawn under Qwikster's existence – it had not even made it into operation. Hastings announced that the services wouldn't change (although the price increase would stay). The justification for the spinoff being reversed was linked back to Facebook's idea that a company in its early days should innovate quickly and in doing so not be concerned if it broke things. 'There is a difference between moving quickly

– which Netflix has done very well for years – and moving too fast, which is what we did in this case,' Hastings said.

A retrospective news report from CNET, published a year later, claimed that, in preparing for Qwikster, Netflix had quickly moved its DVD team to a new building several blocks away from its main offices, managers stopped attending senior meetings and there had been little internal discussion about the botched plan.[10]

The four-month saga had a colossal impact on Netflix. By the time the company revealed its third-quarter earnings it had 800,000 fewer subscribers and its stocks had dropped off a cliff. Around the time of the price increase, before the real impact of subscriber unhappiness had been felt, based on 2019 prices the value of Netflix's shares had hit an all-time high of $42.68. As the scale of the management blunders unfolded – with the apology video and then the product U-turn – the real damage was felt with the price of shares plummeting to around $9.50 each.

'In Wyoming with 10 investors at a ranch/retreat,' Hastings wrote in a Facebook status days after announcing Qwikster. 'I think I might need a food taster. I can hardly blame them.'[11] Overall, the stock drop didn't affect Netflix's overall earnings. It posted higher revenue and income than analysts expected for the third quarter of 2011, but the whole affair was the first time in years that the total number of Netflix subscribers had declined.

At the height of the problems, the TV didn't help. An American TV host and late-night broadcaster, Conan O'Brien, created a spoof of the video, saying it was as easy to return a DVD to Netflix as throwing it out of a car window. *Saturday Night Live* went one step further and recreated Hastings's and Rendich's video – including the teal shirt and mocking the CEO's goatee. During the skit, two actors elaborately created (and quickly cancelled) Netflix and Qwikster spinoffs. Qwikster, Kwickster and Qwickster were featured and each was mockingly dreamed up to host a separate genre of movies.[12]

There was plenty that could be learnt from what happened with Qwikster. Barry Enderwick, who left the company in 2012, says it was one time Hastings made a judgement error. 'That was a prime example of Reed thinking for the first time more about the business and not about what customers would necessarily want,' he said in a phone interview.

During a 2014 talk at the Stanford Graduate School of Business, Hastings looked back at the Qwikster debacle. He told the audience: 'We would have a phrase, "We have to be so aggressive that it makes our skin crawl." So then when the idea of splitting came up, it made our skin crawl.' He now believes that if the company had decided to tell customers about an impending price rise but made the actual change several months later, then things would have gone smoothly.

'We were blinded not to be trapped with DVD,' Hastings recalled. 'We got through it, barely.'

6

DEALING IN DATA

Netflix knows everything you do. As well as being built on movies, documentaries and TV shows, the business is also a technology company, and the contribution innovation has made to its success shouldn't be ignored.

Every time you use Netflix – no matter whether it's on your phone, iPad, laptop or TV – it amasses data about you and your actions. It will record the time of day that you log in or turn the service on, the number of titles that you browse through, searches that are made and importantly what you watch. Every title on Netflix belongs to a number of genres, which can be combined with user behaviour data to build up a larger picture of each profile. (Each account can have multiple profiles.)

Viewing data can also be broken down into how many minutes you watched a show for before pausing, if you made it all the way through what you were watching, whether you watched a small amount and returned to it at a later date and a myriad of other metrics. The prompts Netflix puts at the end of every few episodes of a series – asking whether you're still watching – let it know that you're still engaged. (There's probably some insight it can glean from how long it takes people to say they're still there.)

When Netflix brings together all of this data from more than 150 million subscribers it has a huge amount of information about how people use its platform. The company's algorithms are used to personalise what each user sees. At its simplest level, each time a person opens Netflix the rows of titles that are shown to them are based on previous viewing. The fact that one person is shown choices from 'Critically Acclaimed Witty TV Programmes', 'Docs and Reality TV' and 'Teen TV for BFFs' doesn't mean that everyone is seeing the same thing.

'We look at your viewing history, let's say the last 30 things you watched, and then we find six other Canadians who have almost identical viewing history and then we say what else have those other Canadians enjoyed that you haven't yet seen,' Hastings said in 2013.[1] If you start watching something and give up halfway through a season, Netflix's algorithm will occasionally bring that show back to the top of your screens to see if you're interested in going back and finishing it off.

There are tens of thousands of different rows that can be presented to subscribers. Netflix users generally won't be shown the same combination of rows, but its algorithm is programmed to occasionally display a type of show that someone may not usually watch. After all, humans often have eccentric and unpredictable tastes. One night a romcom may tempt you, when you don't have a habit of watching the genre.

Historically, it was Netflix's algorithms that allowed the company to make use of its huge 100,000-title DVD collection. It launched the personalisation algorithm Cinematch in 2000. When it didn't have enough of the most demanded DVDs in stock to mail to subscribers, the algorithms would suggest other films that could be rented from its back catalogue. The recommendations were one way of circulating the titles that people might not organically be looking for and also acted as a method to stop customers from feeling their choices were always out of stock.

Now Netflix uses the information generated by its customers to help create new shows. 'We start with the data,' Hastings told *Venturebeat* in 2016. 'But the final call is always gut. It's informed intuition.'[2] The year before, he said that data is heavily used in the marketing of its shows, but when it comes to the production process, scripts and story lines, this is left up to the creators of the titles.

When a new 12-episode series launches, Netflix is able to easily see how many people started watching it, the percentage that made it through the first episode, how many people continued watching it and the number who got to the end of the entire series. It can also see how quickly people were watching: did they binge all the episodes in one sitting or watch them more slowly?

Granular data can inform the company whether it should commission a second series. Netflix can also forecast, based on people's interests and preferences, how popular a show may be. 'We do really deep data analysis to find how much a new programme would be viewed, and therefore how much budget we should put behind it,' Hastings told the *Daily Telegraph* in 2016.[3]

The best glimpse of how Netflix considers data came from later in 2016. The company released some high-level findings on how its subscribers watched the first seasons of more than 100 different TV series it was streaming. People generally watch horror and thrillers faster than political dramas and complex shows. Those watching *Breaking Bad* or *The Walking Dead* would typically get through a season in four days and spend more than two hours and 30 minutes a day watching them, Netflix said; whereas *House of Cards* and *Mad Men* took around six days to be finished and under two hours a day was spent watching them. Separate analysis from Netflix has said there's a certain episode in each series – the episode varies by show – that when watched 70 per cent of people went on to complete the entire season.

The result of this is that Netflix users are always being tested. Experiments try to get people watching more shows and viewing them all the way to their end. Every year the company runs hundreds of A/B tests and they can result in different experiences of Netflix. These tests involve different design features, new ways in which information is presented about shows or changes such as how its home screen looks. For the tests, people are split into different groups of 100,000. Each has a different experience and the one that gets the most engagement could be used more widely across Netflix's offering.

The most common type of A/B testing is done around the cards that advertise shows to Netflix subscribers. Each movie, TV series and documentary has a rectangular title card that features an image from the show and its name. There are multiple cards created for each show and these are presented to different subscribers. The ones that get the most people to click and start watching a title are then used more widely. But this is only the tip of the iceberg.

A million-dollar prize

On 2 October 2006, Netflix did something completely new. Amid its price and subscriber battle with Blockbuster, Hastings decided the firm needed to improve the algorithms that underpinned the recommendation systems which were suggesting new films for people to watch.

Instead of investing millions of dollars to hire new computer scientists, the company launched a public competition. 'The Netflix Prize seeks to substantially improve the accuracy of predictions about how much someone is going to love a movie based on their movie preferences,' the website of the contest read.[4]

Developers were tasked with improving the Cinematch algorithm by creating a system that could better predict whether someone would like another movie based on their previous choices. If a person or team could improve the Netflix system by at least 10 per cent, they would win prize money of a million dollars. (The measurement was based on how predicted ratings compared to actual ratings that were made by people.)

'Recommendation systems covering a wide variety of categories will play an increasingly significant commercial role in the future,' Hastings said in a news release. 'Right now, we're driving the Model T version of what is possible. We want to build a Ferrari and establishing the Netflix Prize is a first step.' The contest was inspired by the British government's 1714 Longitude Prize, which asked people how to work out a ship's longitude while at sea.

To encourage engineers, academics and coders to test their algorithms, Netflix also said it would make a huge dataset of 100 million anonymous movie ratings (from one to five stars) available. The ratings were from its overall dataset, which included more than one billion movie ratings. They were collected between 1998 and 2005 and spanned 480,000 different customers and around 18,000 movies.

Customer names and identity numbers were replaced with a new set of randomly assigned codes, and movie details were stripped back to the date the rating was made, its title and the year it was released. Hastings didn't expect the competition to be over quickly. 'It may take months; it might take years,' the prize website read. If nobody reached the 10 per cent improvement in the first year there would be a $50,000 award. The annual prize would be given out for every year the competition went on.

The catch? Netflix made it clear that anyone submitting their entry into the competition would have to share their method, give it to Netflix with a non-exclusive licence, and describe how the results were achieved. (Each entry had to be uploaded to the Netflix Prize website, be within a strict set of rules and requirements, and be verified by an internal Netflix team of judges.)

The prize proved to be instantly popular. Within the first week of the contest being launched Netflix bragged that more than 8,100 teams from 99 countries around the world had signed up. There had even been some early entries: 82 teams submitted their algorithmic systems. Although only one of these had improved on Cinematch's results by 1 per cent (qualifying it for the $50,000 prize if no greater improvements were made within the following year).

To spice up the contest, Netflix also put a leaderboard on its website. Here entrants could see how their algorithm had performed and how it stacked up against the competition. Initial progress was quick. Within a month the top teams had improved on Cinematch's performance by more than 5 per cent. Then progress started to slow and improvements were marginal. By the end of the first year of the competition the improvement had reached 8.44 per cent better than Netflix's offering and the first $50,000 prize went to a team called KorBell – consisting of three engineers working at AT&T's research lab.

The ultimate million-dollar prize was given, in part, to staff working at AT&T. In September 2009 the seven-person team, called BellKor's Pragmatic Chaos, was crowned as the winners of the Netflix Prize. (They decided to split the prize between them according to their own formula.) By the time the competition was nearing its climax, the leading competitors had started to merge their efforts to get across the line. BellKor's Pragmatic Chaos passed the 10 per cent mark in June and in doing so started a 30-day final race to see if anyone could beat it. It was nearly beaten too.

BellKor's Pragmatic Chaos managed to improve on the Cinematch effort by 10.06 per cent. However, another team also hit exactly the same increase. A group called Ensemble narrowly missed out on winning the contest as it submitted its results 20 minutes later than its rival. 'That 20 minutes was worth a million dollars,' Hastings said at a press conference in New York.[5] (The winners took the prize because they were the first to cross the line.)

Hastings, perhaps unsurprisingly, said the contest had been a win for Netflix. As well as getting plenty of free publicity and acting as an advert for the type of work computer scientists could get stuck into, it also made changes to Cinematch because of the results. He told the *New York Times*: 'You look at the cumulative hours and you're getting PhDs for a dollar an hour.'

Yet it was realised very early on that there had been a problem with the Netflix Prize. Researchers looking at the data found they could deanonymise some of the ratings and tie them back to the people who had originally made them.

Academics from the University of Texas found that by comparing rankings of movies and their time-stamps with public data on the online movie database IMDb, it was possible to determine the identity of the person in the supposedly obscured Netflix data. They weren't able to reverse-engineer the entire dataset, just instances where a person had rated movies online as well as within the Netflix information. It was possible to identify someone with just eight movie ratings.[6] Another deanonymisation warning had happened the same year the Netflix Prize started. AOL released 20 million web search queries for researchers to examine, and within weeks the *New York Times* found the identity of users: in one case the person behind the searches 'numb fingers', '60 single men' and 'dog that urinates on everything'.[7]

After the popularity of its first Netflix Prize, Hastings decided the company would run a second one. They were so keen to get it started that the second version was announced the day that BellKor's Pragmatic Chaos were formally declared winners. However, it didn't last.

The data deanonymisation from the first Netflix Prize caught the attention of lawyers and the Federal Trade Commission (FTC). A class action lawsuit filed against Netflix alleged it had broken fair-trade laws when it gave its dataset to researchers. (Video rental records were highly protected in the US after a Supreme Court nominee was previously embarrassed by the publication of his history.)

The second Netflix Prize was planned to have a vastly wider dataset than the original. At the time of the announcement, the *New York Times* said the sequel would include renters' age, gender, ZIP code, genre ratings and previously picked movies. This wealth of personal information would make it potentially a lot easier, and more intrusive, to discover who was behind the DVD choices. It was planned that the second prize – for which computer scientists would predict which movies people would like – would have no accuracy target but $500,000 would be given to the team that was leading after half a year, and then after 18 months the team leading would get another half a million dollars.

However, five months after the second prize had been announced a blog post appeared on Netflix's website and cancelled it. Neil Hunt, a product officer, wrote that Netflix had settled the outstanding lawsuit and come to an agreement with the FTC that would introduce 'certain parameters for how we use Netflix data in any future research programs'. The second prize was cancelled, before it even started.[8] In 2013, Netflix dabbled with a competition again. This time it was even more specialised and aimed at developers who could improve how video was delivered through the internet via cloud computing. The $100,000 prize was split into ten $10,000 awards and handed out at the end of the year.

Hastings, looking back at the prize in a 2018 TED Talk, said the approach was one that worked at the time, and the fact that Netflix hadn't repeated it on a grand scale showed it was 'a very specialised tool'. He said: 'That was a lucky break of good timing rather than a general framework.'[9]

7

A CULTURE OF TRUST

Instead of having a desk the CEO roams around the offices and uses whatever desks are available, plus his laptop and phone, to get things done. It has been the case since around 2008.

Having no fixed station works for Reed Hastings as he is able to visit other members of staff around the company and talk to different people. (If he has specific meetings he will often go to the office of the people he is meeting with or has meeting rooms booked.) 'It makes me more approachable and less imperial,' he told a Berlin media conference in 2015, before joking that not having an office also allows him to leave work early because nobody knows where he is.[1]

The idea of freedom and responsibility is one that's at the heart of how Netflix works. At times, the company describes freedom and responsibility as treating its staff like adults and trusting them. 'Our model is to increase employee freedom as we grow, rather than limit it, to continue to attract and nourish innovative people, so we have a better chance of sustained success,' the original culture deck says.[2]

This means it has adopted a number of policies that other businesses don't even consider. Up until 2004 Netflix had a pretty standard staff holiday policy. Employees were allocated a set number of days' holiday per year. At that point, the culture deck says, a member of staff – who was presumably tired of answering emails late in the evening and working weekends – turned around and said they weren't tracked on how many hours they worked in a day or a week so why is holiday monitored?

Netflix scrapped annual vacation allowances, as a result. Instead the company now lets employees decide how much holiday they take. The obvious drawback is that people may feel pressured to be in the office, work too much, and not take as much holiday as they would if they had set limits. Hastings and senior managers take long breaks to set positive examples for the rest of the company.

Hastings has previously said that he takes six weeks' holiday per year and uses that time to focus on new ideas and what his priorities should be. 'You often do your best thinking when you're off hiking in some mountain or something. You get a different perspective on things,' he said in 2015, according to a *CNBC* report.[3] He's also said he considers the phrase 'work–life balance' the wrong way of thinking. It should be 'work–life integration' instead, whereby employees find the best ways for them to fit work around their other responsibilities in life.

In this regard, Netflix is flexible about how employees want to work. There are no nine-to-five set hours. If a staff member works better in the evening, then they're able to do it. As long as they perform well, it is up to employees to manage their own time. Hastings has said he is quite strict that the company culture should dictate that meetings happen in traditional working hours. 'Ultimately we care about what you get accomplished, not do you also coach your kid's baseball team. Because it is much more about the work, opposed to what hours you put in,' he said while being given an award by Stanford University for leading the entrepreneurial company of the year in 2014.[4]

Netflix's policy on parental leave is similarly generous and can be as much as the parents want. Applying to both mothers and fathers, Netflix offers parents as much time off as they need. (It says people usually take between four and eight months.) Staff are required to work with their managers to figure out how much time they need off and this allows them to ensure the correct cover is organised. Employees can then return on a full-time or part-time basis, and if they need to leave again the option is there for them. During their time off they'll be paid normally.

Employees are also trusted with what they take from Netflix. The company's original culture document explains that people should treat company property as their own and not be overexuberant.

People are expected to 'act in Netflix's best interest'. When travelling, staff should do so as if they were using their own money to pay. (Until at least 2017, Hastings has owned two private jets that he has leased back to Netflix to help with staff travel in the US. Two of the company's major offices, Los Gatos and Los Angeles, are a 350-mile, five-hour drive apart, or a 90-minute flight.)

When Netflix employees are entertaining guests or claiming expenses, the same attitude applies: be mindful of what you're spending but there are no strict limits. 'Expense only what you would otherwise not spend, and is worthwhile for work,' the culture deck says. It also adds that people should only take from Netflix when it is inefficient not to take and inconsequential. The company doesn't mind people making personal calls on work phones or printing personal documents in the office. It doesn't see them as a big loss, and it would be more of a hassle for staff to complete the mundane tasks if they were forced to go elsewhere.

Everyone is responsible

John Ciancutti says the team around Hastings failed to stop him from creating the Qwikster debacle, which could have completely destroyed Netflix. While Hastings apparently doesn't like to rule with top-down decisions, Qwikster was one case where he did. He fully believed that separating the company into a DVD arm and a streaming business was the right thing to do.

'We failed in a sense that we did not lay on railway track,' Ciancutti, who spent more than a decade at the company, says in a phone call. A large number of staff were concerned about the proposal. 'I think our view was basically: Well, I think Reed's crazy on this, but when I disagree with Reed he's right so much more than I am that I'm going to defer to him on this rather than, like, wave a giant red flag and say, "Reed, no."'

Reflecting on Qwikster in 2016, Hastings said the incident was partly because he had been too confident and partly a failing of the culture within the company. 'I realised this is how arrogance happens,' he said during a talk at his old college, Bowdoin. Because he had made a number of correct decisions he started to believe, as the people around him did as well, that he must be right. This type of arrogance started to lower the 'usual threshold of doubt'.[5]

'In hindsight many of my team members said: "I thought it was really stupid but you've been right so much I thought I was wrong and Reed was right,"' Hastings recalled. It taught him one big lesson: 'That my role as leader is to farm for dissent. It's that dissent doesn't happen naturally, deference happens naturally.'

Netflix's culture document is clear that people shouldn't go along with decisions they're unhappy with. 'If you disagree on a material issue, it is your responsibility to explain why you disagree, ideally in both discussion and in writing,' the document says. People who don't agree and fail to speak up are seen as a hindrance to what the company is trying to achieve. Netflix is blunt about this: 'Silent disagreement is unacceptable and unproductive.'

In her book, *Powerful*, Netflix's former HR director, Patty McCord, says on one occasion there was a big disagreement between the company's head of marketing and its head of content. Both had valid points. 'Reed did a beautiful thing,' McCord writes. 'He arranged a debate between the two, onstage, in chairs facing each other, in front of the rest of the executive team.'[6]

The twist was that both had to argue the other's opinion. The format became a regular type of event, McCord says, with people having to debate counterpoints in front of their peers. People would also be asked to break out into smaller groups to try to find solutions to problems that Netflix was facing.

To get people to air their disputes – which they're told to do in constructive ways – Netflix tries to give its employees as much information as possible. 'We're like the anti-Apple, with how they compartmentalise – we're like the opposite,' Hastings said in a 2018 TED Talk. 'Everybody gets all the information. What we're trying to do is build a sense of responsibility in people and the ability to do things.'[7]

Sharing of information goes back to the company's earliest days. Nirmal Srinivasan, in a phone call, says that when she worked in the engineering teams, a huge amount of data was given to her about what Netflix's goals for the coming period were. When Netflix was at its smallest, the company used to attend the local cinema in Los Gatos, where everyone would be told the latest data and priorities for work.

'Nearly every document is fully open for anyone to read and comment on, and everything is cross-linked,' the current Netflix culture document says. 'Memos on each title's performance, on every strategy decision, on every competitor, and on every product feature test are open for all employees to read.' It adds that this means there will be some leaks of its internal information, but they're worth it in exchange for a staff understanding of what they're working towards.

Hastings likes to trust the people around him with their expertise. He leaves the commissioning of shows to the chief content officer, Ted Sarandos, for instance. 'I pride myself on making as few decisions as possible in a quarter,' he said during the TED Talk. 'And we're getting better and better at that. There's some times I can go a whole quarter without making any decisions.' He's said that as Netflix has reached a huge scale he has tried to focus on the company's strategic decisions rather than just those that involve large amounts of money.

Barry Enderwick, who spent more than a decade working at director level within Netflix's marketing teams, says Hastings surrounded himself with a group of staff he could trust to make decisions. He highlights the early roles of the vice-presidents of marketing, operations, content and finance – who later became the chiefs in those areas. 'The impression I got was it was almost like a council of elders,' Enderwick says. 'Reed knew that he didn't know everything about those particular fields. So we went and found people who were very smart and were able to express their understanding and depth of knowledge in those particular fields. He knew what he didn't know and didn't understand or didn't have full control over, and got people who did. Part of being treated like an adult is you're trusted with all this knowledge and you're also trusted to make decisions.'

Enderwick recalls staff within the marketing department being able to sign cheques for multimillion-dollar advertising campaigns, and these wouldn't need to be signed off by the chief marketing officer, or by Hastings. (In March 2019, after the firm's chief marketing officer of six years, Kelly Bennett, stepped down, the company dissolved its entire global marketing team.)

The company's culture document says that internally a lot of time is spent debating strategy, and once the general principles have been formed it is then up to the individual teams, who have the specific expertise, to get to the final results.

'Incredible people don't want to be micromanaged,' Hastings said at Stanford University in 2014.[8] Instead the company decides to encourage managers to provide context about the work that they're doing. They're told not to make top-down decisions or rely on committees. Instead, they are encouraged to follow the strategies, provide transparency around choices, and make other staff members understand why what they're doing should be the right approach.

'The idea is that we manage through setting context and letting people run,' Hastings said. 'You've got to have the right people, you've got to reinforce that with values, setting context about what the company is trying to achieve.' And when someone does do something stupid, managers are told to think about what information they failed to give to get the results they had wanted.

The context provided to staff can be wide-ranging. 'What are we trying to do, what are the constraints, is it a really big problem or a little problem, must it be done right or do we do an approximate version and fix later?' Hastings said in a talk with Reid Hoffman in 2015 describing the different scenarios provided to staff. 'If you get good at setting context, then you don't have to direct the micro-specifics. There's context about the problem and there's context about behaviour.'[9]

When it comes to the process of making decisions, multiple people are involved. For each significant decision Netflix takes there's someone responsible for making the final call. It's their job to listen to all the views and take the position that they think is correct. 'The bigger a decision, the more extensive the dissent/assent gathering should be, usually in an open shared document,' the company's culture document says. 'We are clear, however, that decisions are not made by a majority or committee vote.'

'The decision-making is pushed deep down into the organisation. He prefers not to make decisions himself,' explains Adrian Cockcroft, who spent six years at the company. He says people were guided to be doing the right thing within loose frameworks of their goals, rather than having set methods to achieve their goals.

He is one of a number of former staff members who say Hastings can be described as using a 'trust, but verify' approach. The phrase originates from a Russian proverb: '*Doveryai no proveryai.*' However, it was popularised when President Ronald Reagan adapted it for use during Cold War negotiations with Russia during the 1980s. For Hastings, the approach works by his trusting his staff with their decisions, but the verification is the results they get.

Overall, the CEO is keen that Netflix doesn't have too many fixed processes in place – as demonstrated by its vacation, expenses and parental-leave policies. His original culture deck described bad processes as being things that constrain people from doing their work. This included: people having to get pre-approval for spending $5,000, needing permission to hang a poster on a wall, multi-level approval for projects and having ten people interview each potential new employee.

There are some processes, though. These include letting colleagues know when code is being updated and making sure spending is within the pre-defined budgets. Meetings are one process that isn't neglected. 'We have a regular cadence of many types of meetings; we start and end on time, and have well-prepared agendas,' the current culture document states. Netflix says the meetings are usually to learn from different people and set context, rather than for decisions to be made.

'Reed created this environment that really inspired people to educate themselves way beyond the norm, so that when we came into those meetings, we were super-prepared,' says Mitch Lowe, one of Netflix's early vice-presidents, who went on to run the cinema ticket subscription company MoviePass. 'He just created this amazing, inspirational environment.'

The purpose of a lack of processes is to learn from the mistakes Hastings made at Pure Software and be flexible to change. Pure followed the rulebook – there were plenty of policies and there was lots of process that had to be followed by staff members.

'Every time someone made a mistake we tried to put a process in place to make sure that mistake didn't happen again,' he told TED's audience. 'The problem is, we were trying to dummy-proof the system and then eventually only dummies wanted to work there.' So when the most popular coding language changed from C and C++, Hastings argued, the company wasn't able to quickly adapt and shift how it worked. This resulted in a slower financial period and it eventually being purchased. With Netflix, once it was proved the company would have some longevity, he wanted to do things differently. After Qwikster, Hastings also said he was 'so obsessed' with not being similar to Kodak or AOL – both arguably missed big industry shifts – that he pressed for streaming too quickly.

A repeat of the fear of being left behind is inherent in Netflix's current culture document. It states that mistakes are tolerated within the company as most of the time they can be recovered from. Hastings believes that innovation happens when people aren't scared of making errors. 'We are in a creative business, not a safety-critical business. Our big threat over time is lack of innovation, so we should be relatively error tolerant.'

Big decisions

Mark Zuckerberg has always had time for Reed Hastings. 'Reed is an entrepreneur and technologist who has led Netflix to transform the way people watch movies and TV,' the Facebook CEO said in June 2011 as he appointed Hastings to the company's board of directors. He praised Hastings for creating a 'culture of continuous rapid innovation' and at other points has said he's acted as a brilliant mentor to him.

Hastings sat on Facebook's board from 2011 to 2019 and also served on Microsoft's board from 2007 to 2012. He stayed in the role at Facebook even during Zuckerberg's increased efforts to make the social network a home for online video. (Hastings reportedly tried to resign from the board after an email he sent to Peter Thiel saying Thiel's support for Donald Trump during the 2016 US presidential election was 'catastrophically bad judgement'.)[10]

But Netflix and Facebook are very different companies. Zuckerberg's offering is free, makes billions of dollars through advertising revenues, and relies upon people sharing their personal data, photos and videos, while Netflix doesn't have ads, charges people every month, and makes its own videos. When Hastings joined Zuckerberg's board there were 23 million Netflix subscribers and Facebook had around 750 million users. At the point of writing, Netflix has 150 million paying customers and Facebook has more than two billion people using its service every month.

As well as their business strategies, the leadership styles of Zuckerberg and Hastings are very different, says John Ciancutti. He has worked for both of the CEOs, first spending 12 years at Netflix in the engineering teams working on the company's video recommendation and personalisation systems, then for a year as director of engineering at Facebook.

Zuckerberg is well known for his central glass office where employees regularly come to meet with him. It's here where he approves decisions and devises the changes that will be made to the Facebook app, plus his suite of Instagram, WhatsApp and Messenger software. With each set of engineers attempting to bend his ear.

'With Reed, if he had a strong view on a product choice, what he would say is: "Let's test it." He would never tell a product manager: "You can't do X, you have to do Y,"' Ciancutti says in a phone call. If there was a disagreement, Hastings would say both options should be tested and the one that worked the best was more likely to be adopted. 'There was a strong testing culture which Reed really helps drive and really utilise to influence the product in a way that was not as top-down as other companies can be.'

There are some similarities in management style between Hastings and Zuckerberg. They both have chosen to host weekly meetings, on a Friday afternoon, to tell employees (some in person but most by video feed) about upcoming announcements and answer the most popular questions submitted by staff.

Nirmal Srinivasan joined Netflix in 2000 as a senior software engineer within the marketing team. By the time she left 14 years later she had worked across all areas of the firm's billing and subscription service. In the early years she says Hastings used to know all of his employees well and take an interest in what they were working on. He stopped by desks occasionally to ask questions about what was happening and could be there for up to 15 minutes delving into the intricacies of the business.

'His mind and hands would be there in everything,' she says during an interview. 'Nothing was unimportant for him.' Over her time at the company Hastings became more confident in his abilities and decision-making. A number of Hastings's former staff and colleagues have described him as being confident in his ability to control the company. They say he's charismatic, articulates his arguments well, and, while never being bad at it, has improved at public speaking as time has gone on.

'When your leader makes the right choice most of the time, not all of the time, you start believing in this,' she says. 'That's what I think Reed Hastings embodied, you could go by his track record. Investing in the unpopular things when he believed it was right.' One key example for her was when Netflix decided to move its website and streaming service to Amazon's infrastructure.

Through Amazon Web Service (AWS), a cloud hosting provider, the company runs its website and streaming technology remotely. Amazon deals with the demand for viewing and the data centre capacity needed, while Netflix focuses on its service. Netflix started to use AWS around 2009, and Srinivasan says the decision to move to AWS came from Hastings.

She says it was a top-down decision from him and it wasn't one that all the engineering staff thought was correct at the time. 'Nobody believed it, a lot of people didn't like it, we all did it,' she says, adding that in hindsight it was the correct decision to make. Now Netflix uses AWS for all of its service – although the video is delivered through its own Open Connect network – and Hastings plus his executives have appeared on stage at Amazon's technology industry conferences talking up its usefulness.

Obviously, Hastings isn't always right with big decisions. Throughout 20 years of running a company not everything will go smoothly. The culture he's built has resulted in the majority of its controversies being kept within its walls, with very few details being leaked. The most startling error was Qwikster. It is also possible there haven't been as many scandals surrounding Netflix as other big technology companies – such as Google and Facebook – because the work it does is more benign. Making movies and TV shows isn't a particularly contentious business and there's little personal data that can be abused or mis-sold. Although in recent years Netflix hasn't shied away from difficult issues. The series *13 Reasons Why* has depicted suicide and sexual abuse – which some commentators deemed too graphic. The show's creators have argued it is shining a light on real-world events. Separately Netflix, along with Disney, has threatened to pull its production teams from Georgia, in the US, after it proposed to introduce repressive abortion laws.

But his former staff say when making huge calls he has often been right. He moved into streaming at the correct time and the U-turn on Netflix not producing its own hardware was the sensible decision too. Tom Dillon, Netflix's chief operations officer between 1999 and 2006, says Hastings let his senior staff be responsible for achieving their goals. 'Reed said: "You're the guy that's running this, I expect you to make the right decision,"' he explained in an interview. For regular one-on-one meetings, which happened weekly but during busy times could be several times a week, Hastings would go to Dillon's office, where they would chat through their priorities.

Dillon describes Hastings as methodical and very analytical, and how he would expect his staff to be thinking of all possible solutions to the tasks they were working on: 'He forced you to really examine every option.' If you hadn't looked at all the available choices, Hastings would inevitably suggest one of them himself and it would invariably be right, he says in a phone interview. John Ciancutti, who spent 12 years at Netflix and climbed to vice-president level, echoed this:

'You work on what you're responsible for all day, every day. All you think about is your job, and then you'll have a monthly one-on-one with Reed, and he will have some insight. This is a thing he thinks about for an hour every month and he's going to have an insight and you're like: Why did I not think of that? Why did I not anticipate that?'

Dillon adds: 'He also didn't suffer fools very well. In other words, if you got into a meeting with Reed and were starting to say things that were obviously stupid, he would pretty much call you out on it.'

Hastings has clear views on what a company's strategy should be. 'The thing most people don't understand about strategy is that strategy is pain,' he said during a conference run by the *New Yorker* in 2016.[11] According to Hastings, a business strategy shouldn't involve safe planning and decision-making that's focused on what will happen over the coming weeks, months and years.

Instead, he says, a strategy should be something that isn't easy. 'If your strategy is not profoundly painful to you and uncomfortable you're not being very strategic.' During the talk he used a militaristic metaphor to describe pain. He said that if you're dominant and in control, with more forces than an opponent, then you don't need to be strategic as you'll be in a position to win whatever happens.

Someone who doesn't have huge resources has to be strategic, Hastings argues. This essentially means that strategy is taking risks and making decisions that may not pay off. 'Really, strategy is a list of all the things you're not doing,' Hastings said. For Netflix, he says, this means sports and pay-per-view television. He argued that the company could do these things but it has strategically decided not to and instead to focus on the key areas of TV and movies.

8

GLOBAL DOMINANCE

On the morning of 6 January 2016, deep within the extravagant Venetian hotel in Las Vegas, Hastings looked pleased with himself. Taking to the stage in the packed, 7,500-capacity, Palazzo Ballroom, the CEO wore a familiar ensemble: a pair of dark jeans, a belt, lilac shirt and blazer. As is often customary with his public appearances, Hastings quickly zipped through the history of television. The 'miracle' of black-and-white broadcast TV starting in the mid-1930s, the invention of VHS tapes, and finally the creation of on-demand streaming.

'Internet TV allows us to define what is possible,' he confidently said, extolling the power of allowing customers to be able to click and watch what they want, when they want.[1] The first 40 minutes of the press conference, taking place at the annual Consumer Electronics Show, were relatively dull. Hastings painstakingly detailed the growth of Netflix's success, starting from its introduction of streaming in 2007 to its then 74 million subscribers. He then handed the stage to his chief of content, Ted Sarandos, who hosted a panel discussion with some of Netflix's actors.

Yet the day was due to be one of the most significant in Netflix's time in streaming and a crucial one for its continued survival. After the panel discussion, Hastings appeared back on stage for the event's final five minutes, standing in front of a screen constantly rotating through still images of what it considered to be its biggest shows so far: *Orange Is the New Black, House of Cards, Narcos, Jessica Jones*.

With growing pace, he changed course. 'While we have been here on stage at CES, we switched Netflix on in Azerbaijan,' Hastings said. 'In Vietnam,' he continued, deliberately speaking in short, staccato, sentences. 'In India. In Nigeria. In Poland. In Russia. In Saudi Arabia. In Singapore. In South Korea. In Turkey. In Indonesia and 130 new countries.' Behind the scenes engineers at Netflix had completed the final stage of a global rollout. While Hastings spoke, his company had increased the locations in which it was available to 190 countries. It's now available everywhere except China, the Republic of Crimea in Russia, North Korea and Syria. People started to notice instantly, with Reuters tweeting a breaking-news announcement that Netflix was available in India before it had been said on stage.

But Hastings's grand plan to be available everywhere in the world was a long time in the making. Sometime around

2004–5, Hastings was planning his first international expansion. At the time, there was no streaming service and the company was solely focused on renting DVDs to its customers in the US. The United Kingdom was set to be the firm's second destination. At the time, Blockbuster, Screenselect and Lovefilm were dominant in the UK's rental market.

Hastings wasn't just thinking about the launch: plans had advanced to a point where it was imminent. Tom Dillon, Netflix's former chief operations officer, was heavily involved in the project to move the company's DVD service abroad for the first time.

'I went over to the UK to start up the operations and I had rented a warehouse, hired staff, we had bought all the movies,' he says during an interview. Netflix's staff, he says, had conducted an analysis of where in the UK was the best place to allow a high number of customers to get discs within one day of ordering them. The centre of the UK was picked.

Then Hastings pulled the plans and Netflix stayed only in the US. Dillon says: 'We were literally a few days away from going live and we decided to completely abandon the UK because of the rumour, or our belief, that Amazon were going to jump in, in the US, and that we needed all of our resources to focus on fighting Amazon.'

International expansion was put on hold for a number of years. In hindsight the move was probably correct; the logistical growth for DVDs far outweighs the capabilities needed for a widely used streaming service. (Dillon says not launching in the UK was the right call from Hastings.) DVDs required quality checking, packing and constant replacement when they were damaged – as well as the physical space and staff (or robots) needed to perform these tasks. Ultimately the rumours of an Amazon rental launch could have saved Netflix from a DVD-shaped headache in an increasingly competitive market.

It was only years later, when Netflix had a more established footing, that Hastings did return to international expansion. By April 2010 the company had amassed 14 million subscribers and it set out to hire a director of product management to lead the international growth. At this point the company had been streaming for three years and had ironed out some of the clunkiness in its system – although it was far from perfect.

Hastings picked Canada for the first non-US streaming launch and started there in September 2010 (with a price of $7.99 a month). Almost instantly the inevitable problem of streaming rights raised its head: commentators cautioned that while the first three series of *Mad Men* were available, the fourth wasn't; and, unlike in the US version of Netflix, there weren't any episodes of *Glee*.

The launch didn't exactly go to plan either. Journalists found out the company had hired extras to attend its press event and given them a script to talk up how much they were excited about the launch of Netflix. A spokesperson for the company apologised. And then Hastings committed a rare public misstep. Jokingly, he responded to a question from the *Hollywood Reporter* about Canadian streaming being

$1 cheaper than US streaming with the response: 'How much has it been your experience that Americans follow what happens in the world? It's something we'll monitor, but Americans are somewhat self-absorbed.'[2] A day later he called the comment 'awkward' in a blog post and said sorry.

After Canada, international expansion came quickly: 43 Latin American countries were next in 2011, then the UK, France, Germany, Austria, Switzerland, Belgium, Luxembourg, plus Australia and New Zealand before the mass rollout from the Venetian in 2016.

To make it possible to stream in almost 200 countries around the world, Netflix has created its own infrastructure. Working with internet providers it has installed its Open Connect boxes in data centres. These systems act as localised caches of Netflix: during the non-peak watching hours Open Connect will download what Netflix's algorithms predict the majority of people in each location will want to watch. Then each is ready to stream as soon as the play button is hit.

When Netflix's 130-country expansion happened, *WIRED* reported that the company did this from four Open Connect boxes.[3] These were situated in Dubai, Singapore, Hong Kong and Johannesburg. Now Netflix has increased the amount of subscribers it has in its global market, the number of Open Connect boxes has also shot up. There are currently thousands of the boxes around the world and they deliver 100 per cent of Netflix's video content to viewers.

There's one big location that doesn't have any Open Connect boxes, though: China. The Communist nation is the biggest country in the world and there's no version of Hastings's streaming service available. The company has never been able to 'crack' China and its potential 1.3 billion subscribers.

It's a market that other major tech firms want to break into: in recent years it has been reported that both Facebook and Google have been working to create filtered versions of their services to get around Chinese bans. When Google's efforts, dubbed Project Dragonfly, were revealed by an investigative news website, *The Intercept*, in 2018, there was a huge staff backlash at the firm, saying censorship didn't fit in with its principles.[4] The problems are the strict rules and censorship that the country's government requires to keep its regime going. If companies can't ensure Chinese moderators will approve their content, then the whole company won't be granted a business licence.

Hastings has long been keen on Netflix entering the Chinese market, but the company hasn't found an official way to launch its streaming there. In 2015 Hastings said Netflix was working to create a 'modest' service in China. A year later, in an interview with the tech website *Recode*, Hastings said the company had been talking with China's internet regulator, SARFT, to build up a relationship.[5] This ultimately didn't amount to anything. 'We probably assessed it wrong,' Hastings said at *Recode*'s annual conference in 2017. 'We had our natural optimism, which slowly got beat down.'[6]

Hastings hasn't completely given up on China, though. Instead of launching a heavily stymied version of Netflix there, it has opted to sell video through licensing. Towards the end of April 2017 the company struck a deal with the video platform iQiyi, which is owned by the tech giant Baidu, to make some of its Originals series available. The 'expectations of our deal are modest in scope', Netflix said on its website and it name-checked *Stranger Things* and *Black Mirror* as two shows that may be broadcast to Chinese viewers.[7]

And continuing its China push in 2017, Netflix also announced it had commissioned its first Chinese-language Original, a prison break series called *Bardo* (擺渡身) that, like all of its other Originals, was made available to every streaming subscriber. The company has also been buying the rights to some shows from iQiyi and fellow Chinese production house YouKu Tudou, which is owned by Alibaba. So while it's not allowed to operate in China as a stand-alone service, Netflix isn't about to totally lose out on Chinese-language speakers.

Rise of the Originals

Open Netflix and you'll be greeted with a volley of viewing options – most people browse around 40–50 titles before they pick what they're going to watch. Each show is represented by a rectangular card that when selected starts playing a short trailer to entice a potential viewer to select the show. Seemingly endless rows of shows appear and there'll often be unconventional genres available: Escapist Reality TV, Women Who Rule the Screen, Wine & Beverage Appreciation and Brain Food Docs are just a few of them.

The varied genres exist to group people by categories and present them with the programming they may want to watch. Hastings has said the ideal scenario would see every customer presented with a few shows that they consider must-watches. (Unfortunately, human moods are a little more complex than that.)

Within each genre, and most evidently in the largest ones, a change has happened. Now when you scroll through the list of possible viewing there will increasingly be one common theme: in the top-right corner of the display card will be the bright-red Netflix logo, standing proudly over the content.

The overt branding is to tell you, in no uncertain terms, that you're planning on watching a Netflix Original. The term is cloaked in some mystery as what it's defined as involves a few different interpretations. Shows that Netflix has produced or co-produced are counted as Originals, but also those that Netflix has purchased exclusive rights to. What's an Original in one country may not be in another.

Hastings and Netflix started to experiment with Originals before the company had reached any significant scale. 'We tried it early in 2005 on the DVD basis, we only had five million subscribers,' Hastings told a Stanford University class in 2015.[8]

One of the first original pieces of programming Netflix

was involved in was the first film by the independent creators Mark and Jay Duplass. Hastings had given Ted Sarandos, his chief content officer, who oversaw DVD purchases at the time, a small budget of around $100,000 to sign and boost the profile of promising films and documentaries he found at the Sundance Film Festival, the annual Salt Lake City gathering of the indie film scene.

Sarandos's earliest picks included the Duplass brothers' *The Puffy Chair* – a $15,000 shoestring creation charting the relationships between family and friends. Under the guise of Red Envelope Entertainment, Netflix started to distribute more than 100 indie films exclusively. The division had some early hits: it distributed DVDs of *Born into Brothels*, a film exploring the lives of prostitutes and their children in Calcutta six months before it won an Oscar for Best Documentary, and the romcom *Nice Guys Sleep Alone*. Through its recommendation system Netflix was able to expose the new, unheard-of titles to its subscribers who had shown similar tastes.

Sarandos had grand ambitions for Red Envelope Entertainment, telling *WIRED*: 'Eventually we'll be coming to Sundance and saying, "We can buy everything. There's a deal for every film."'[9] After the successes, Netflix planned to start funding the production of new titles. However, this didn't go to plan. In 2008, Red Envelope was canned – it was employing around 50 people. The reason for shutting the service? Netflix said it was 'running into our studio partners' in the meetings where it was buying rights to films and TV shows.

Months before its Qwikster troubles in 2011, Hastings

took the gamble to go back into original programming. If the company could create new shows that it solely owned the rights to, then it would be less reliant on purchasing licences for other titles. It was a huge gamble, but with an increasing focus on its streaming business, the company needed more shows it could offer to all of its subscribers at once.

On 6 February 2012, an entire year before the political thriller *House of Cards* debuted, Hastings's first Original was released. *Lilyhammer* was set in the small Norwegian town of Lillehammer and was intended to be a spinoff from *The Sopranos*. Steven Van Zandt, who had played Silvio Dante in the mobster show, was the lead character.

One of *Lilyhammer*'s first reviews came from the *Hollywood Reporter*, which gave it faint praise – calling it an 'odd little series with potential'.[10] Most of the review's criticism was directed at the placing of Van Zandt's character in Norway; it was said he didn't seem at home and there was confusion around how much of the language his character understood. While *Lilyhammer* may have been important as an initial experiment and helped to pave the way for *House of Cards*, it did introduce a new concept. Netflix made all of the initial eight episodes available at the same time, something it now does with the vast majority of its series.

Despite the show's inconsistencies it ended up running for three seasons. But the *Hollywood Reporter's* initial review did make one crucial observation: 'If the rental/streaming service is ever going to become a serious threat to networks or cable channels, it will not only need a lot more offerings, but a lot better ones as well.'

House of Cards was Netflix's first real challenge to the established TV networks. The company splashed $100m on an initial two seasons. It was a huge risk but Netflix was confident it would perform well based on the data it had and it backed this up by opening its chequebook. Hastings has said the company 'paid way more than anyone is supposed to pay' for the initial rights. At the time the company was bidding against HBO for the Kevin Spacey show. In a rare move Netflix read the show's entire script, compared it to the original British version, and commissioned two series. The model broke the traditional approach of commissioning a pilot episode and testing it on audiences before committing to a full TV series.

'It was a large part of our budget,' Hastings told a media conference in Berlin in 2015. 'We debated it back and forth, we almost didn't do it, we thought what if we can't pay for this because the business doesn't grow?'[11] Despite the huge outlay, Sarandos convinced Hastings that 2010 was the right time to start investing in TV series as the company was already spending a huge amount of money on the rights to stream shows.

It was the right decision for him to back. In 2018, Netflix spent $12bn on content and planned to have produced 1,000 Originals by the end of the year. There are a couple of reasons why Originals worked after 2012 (when *Lilyhammer* was released) compared to the closure of Red Envelope four years earlier.

The first: streaming had taken off. Secondly, Netflix had reached a critical mass. By 2013, when the first season of

House of Cards premiered, Hastings's business had reached 44 million subscribers across the world, and its customers were predominantly watching shows online rather than renting DVDs (which was only ever possible in the United States). Netflix's ownership of the rights for its Originals means it can launch them simultaneously in every country it operates in. It doesn't have to enter country-level negotiations and pay to be able to make one of its own shows available there. There are also the limited distribution costs of streaming when compared to the Originals Netflix released on DVD during the mid-2000s.

Hastings has given Sarandos credit for the Originals strategy and commissioning. The track record of popular shows Netflix has produced indicates that its method works. Among the most hyped have been *Orange Is the New Black*, *Stranger Things*, *The Crown*, *GLOW*, Marvel's *Daredevil*, and the reinvention of Charlie Brooker and Annabel Jones's *Black Mirror*, which it nabbed from the UK's Channel 4. Despite the hits, there have been plenty of complete flops that have failed to be renewed beyond a first season.

The production and commissioning of hundreds of shows would be too much for Sarandos to manage on his own. In keeping with Netflix's cultural values of giving freedom and responsibility to its staff, there are a number of executives who can commission new shows. Sarandos gives them the same trust Hastings allows him. 'My direct-report team can greenlight any project without my approval,' he told the movie magazine *Vulture* in 2018.[12] There are some budget restraints, he says. It's more likely he will be involved in discussions about series that will cost around $10m per episode than those with a $3m budget.

Historically, Netflix has refused to reveal the number of people watching its shows. Hastings has said it is more interested in people getting to the end of shows than the overall number of people who watch them. But in early 2019 it started to change its approach. A letter to shareholders in January said the original series *You* and *Sex Education* were both set to be watched by 40 million households in their first four weeks, its horror movie *Bird Box* was said to be viewed by at least 80 million households and the Spanish Original *Elite* was watched by 20 million households in its first month. It followed this up in July 2019 by saying 40.7 million accounts started watching the third season of *Stranger Things* in the first four days after it was released. It also said its film *Murder Mystery* had 30.9 million viewers over its first three days.

Netflix has been very selective in releasing the few viewing figures it has made available. It has only done it for a few specific shows – presumably the Originals that have been the biggest successes – and continued not to provide viewership figures for the rest of its shows. While there are now more than 150 million paying accounts on Netflix, the company has estimated through its use of multiple profiles per account that there are at least 300 million people who use its service.

Netflix hasn't publicised any numbers for the shows that may be considered unsuccessful or ones it doesn't renew for extra seasons. The company has confirmed it counts a view as someone who got more than 70 per cent of the way into a show or movie, but the figures are still fairly vague and not verified by an independent party.

But, for Hastings, how many people watch Originals counts as only one measure of success. The business thrives on subscribers and if it makes shows people will discuss (either on social media or face to face), then it is likely to tempt new people to sign up for an account. People don't want to miss out on huge cultural moments and are willing to sign up to Netflix to be part of them.

When asked what he thought about people who signed up for a Netflix account but barely watched the service, he said the company needs to make more shows they want to watch, then it will get more success. 'Over time you will stay with us longer and you will evangelise us to your friends if you're watching the shows,' he said. 'Watching on Netflix is a habit. If some piece of content gets you to try it again then you'll start using it and watching it more and more.'

Reflecting on its Originals and the decision to start producing them, Hastings summed up the company's position: 'It's really about making the brand stronger so that more people want to join and *House of Cards* absolutely did that. Many people would talk about it and associate that brand with us.'

Tackling spiralling debt

Creating movies and TV shows is costly – and Hastings knows it. Since Netflix's push into producing and paying for Originals in 2011 with *Lilyhammer*, the company has completely changed how its financing works. Instead of buying hoards of DVDs, spending money on postal charges and running warehouses shipping millions of discs per day, the company is focused on negotiating the rights to broadcast content as well as paying for the production of entirely new video.

Every year it now spends billions of dollars on the titles that are spread across its service. Financial documents show it spent around $12bn on content during 2018, which included the shows it was producing and co-producing plus licensing for the titles it was buying the rights to. The figure has been growing each year since *Lilyhammer* was made – 2018's figure was a jump of 35 per cent from the year before – and throughout 2019 analysts predicted it would spend in the region of $15bn on shows.

As is the industry standard with movie and TV studios, it's rare for the budgets of individual series or films to be publicly revealed and it's the same for how much the celebrity talent gets paid. There have been a few limited disclosures and reports from industry sources about how much Netflix pays its stars.

One thing is clear: Netflix pays extremely well for the movies and TV shows it makes and has on its platform. Hastings has said the company paid $100m for the first two seasons of *House of Cards*, the first ten episodes of *Marco Polo* (which was cancelled after two series) were said to have cost $90m, and comedian Dave Chappelle is said to have struck a $60m deal for a series of stand-up specials. And at the end of 2018 it was reported that Netflix had paid around $100m to keep all ten seasons of *Friends* streaming for one extra year before the deal with the owners of the rights, Warner Media, expired.

There is no obviously public structure outlining how much Netflix will pay celebrities or the creators of its shows. The company faced criticism in January 2018 from actress and comedian Mo'Nique for one of its alleged offers. In an Instagram post she said her fans should boycott Netflix after she claims she was offered $500,000 to tape a special show for the firm. She says the company allegedly paid Amy Schumer $13m and $20m to both Chris Rock and Dave Chappelle for their comedy specials.

The spending puts Netflix in a complex financial position. It has had to keep paying for new shows and licences to continue attracting customers, but in the process it has accumulated vast debts. It has been spending faster than it has been taking in cash. This position worries some investors and those on Wall Street who fear that the company's bubble will eventually burst before it can make more than it spends.

Hastings has said he's against keeping massive amounts of money. 'I think it's horrible how mismanaged most Silicon Valley companies are in capital,' he said in a talk at Kleiner Perkins Caufield & Byers in 2015.[13] 'They store capital. Let's do the Microsoft example: it always wanted to have a lot of cash on hand, Apple had no cash 15 years ago, who did the most innovation? The cash does not help. The cash insulates you in a bad way.' He went on to say that he believes it is inefficient for companies to keep huge cash reserves and that one reason why they often do so is because it helps to please their boards, who don't want the business to go bankrupt.

Overall, at the end of 2018 the company had a negative cash flow of $3bn for the entire year. It was the fifth year in a row that the company burnt cash it didn't have. Netflix has been raising more debts to pay for its bills too. In the final quarter of 2018 it raised around $2bn in extra debt to help finance its future growth. During the last five years the company has raised several rounds of debt.

And over the coming years it will have to start paying these back. Netflix will owe $32bn for shows it has been commissioning, debt repayments and other operating costs. Many of the deals it has made to create new shows haven't required payment up front, but they will eventually have to be accounted for. The company has been upfront about the fact that its strategy is to capitalise on its giant market share while it can and attract new customers with even more popular shows. That strategy has continued. The company says it expected to have a negative cash flow of $3bn during 2019.

Hastings hopes that in the coming years the company will have grown enough to reduce the gap between the money it gets through subscriptions and the amount it spends on content every year. Higher numbers of subscribers will mean the company has an even larger market share in the streaming world and, importantly, will have guaranteed levels of income. During a company earnings call at the end of October 2018, Hastings disputed whether the negative $3bn figure was the company losing money. 'You're using the word loss and I think you mean the investment,' he said.[14] He sees the firm spending more money than it has as helping to build its future. It's an ongoing cycle where new shows that create a hype are needed to attract new subscribers, but for the creation of the shows there needs to be money that's available to spend.

'Netflix is approaching a point where the growth in operating profit is going to grow faster than our growth in content cash spend. And that's really going to drive the free cash flow towards improvement,' added the company's chief finance officer, David Wells, who left the company at the start of 2019. Wells said the cash flow would 'eventually break even', although he didn't put a date on it, beyond saying there'll be improvements by 2020. 'We still think it's going to be a few years towards breakeven because we're optimizing again for long-term cash flow and long-term profitability, and we think that's the right thing.'

Conquering the world

Raja Harishchandra is the story of a royal figure who won't be corrupted. The 40-minute film sees King Harishchandra banished from his own empire, and almost simultaneously his son dies. But at the end of the silent, black-and-white movie all of his hardship was revealed to be a test by his God.

After being released in 1913 – it is credited as one of India's first movies – it helped to kickstart a nation of film addicts. Every year around 1,500–2,000 films, spanning more than 20 languages, are made and produced in India. Box office takings in the country are set to hit $3.7bn by 2020, and the country's population of 1.5 billion has increasingly become a target for the world's biggest technology companies.

Mark Zuckerberg's encrypted messaging platform WhatsApp has its largest market in India, with more than 400 million users, and the wider Facebook company has attempted to provide free internet connections to parts of the country. (Legal challenges forced it to change its offering, after saying it was anti-competitive.)

Netflix has similar ambitions in India. Hastings told media in the country that he can see the next 100 million of his subscribers coming from the nation. 'Most people in the world do not have a passport and so it is critical for us at Netflix to build a sense of community in them towards other people around the world,' Hastings told the *Economic Times* Global Business Summit in New Delhi in 2018. 'Stories travel and, unlike an expensive Samsung phone or an iPhone, most people can afford YouTube, Hotstar, Netflix etc. where they can watch these stories unfold.'[15] In a separate interview he said: 'And as with everything in India, even the niche is bigger than most countries.'

In part, the stories Netflix wants to tell are set in India. They're also based in every other country where Netflix has a presence. And that's where it will take Originals through the company's next decade. During the last five years, Hastings has seen slowing and limited growth in the United States. The last quarter of 2018 saw 8.8 million new subscribers join Netflix and the majority of these were from outside the United States (7.3 million international subscribers and 1.5 million from within the country). In many ways, Netflix's large market penetration in the US meant international expansion – which was almost fully completed in 2016 – was inevitable. But it has followed this with international programming. 'We started as Hollywood to the world, because of where we are,' Hastings said in 2018. But this has changed. 'The company is becoming a way to curate some of the world's best storytellers and to share their content everywhere.'[16]

International Originals allow Netflix to appeal to people in its growing markets as local shows can feel more relevant to viewers. Since it went fully global there's been an aggressive push to make shows outside the US, and to use production teams, directors and casts that also aren't US-centric.

The company has commissioned Originals in India, Mexico, Spain, Italy, Germany, Brazil, Turkey and more. Two original movies have already been released in India, with more being produced. In its quest for 'local but global' shows, the unusual – but logical – step of dubbing international shows into English has been taken. It's something that's rarely done in the TV industry but helps Netflix find bigger audiences for its productions. Where possible it's also using the original actors to provide the voices for their own dubbing, with executives saying that provides a more authentic experience.

The strategy, based on Netflix's limited release figures, can work. It's previously said that more than 90 per cent of the viewers of *Dark*, a gritty German series that sees children vanish from a small village, have come from outside the country. And more than half the views of the Brazilian show *3%* originate from other countries.

'Our International Originals can be important to specific countries and regions and also play well outside of their home markets,' the firm said in a letter to shareholders. Netflix also hopes more international content will help it avoid the wrath of regulators. The company has clashed with the Cannes Film Festival in France. It pulled out of the event after the rules were changed to say that only productions that have been released in French cinemas will be eligible for the competition. At the same time, the EU is working on new regulations that will require streaming platforms to produce a certain amount of its content that's available to watch in Europe.

At a French media conference held in Lille in 2018, Hastings said he isn't against regulation and that it's Netflix's job to 'participate, to figure out and follow those regulations'. He said: 'I know at times we have a reputation as a disrupter and sometimes we make mistakes.'[17]

The company has shown that it's willing to work with regulators around the world. At the start of 2019, Netflix along with other broadcasters signed a 'Code of best practices for online curated content providers' in India.

Critics have said that the code amounts to censorship of freedom of speech and artistic creation. They argue that the rules prohibit streaming companies – Amazon Prime didn't sign the document – from making comments that could be deemed disrespectful to India or the country's religious beliefs.

At the same time Saudi Arabia censored an episode of the comedy show *Patriot Act with Hasan Minhaj*, which was critical of the country's crown prince. Netflix took the episode down from its service after a request from one of Saudi Arabia's government ministries. As Netflix continues to experiment with new shows and formats, creating them around the world, Hastings is bound to face more situations where governments try to control its output and censor shows they don't agree with.

However, he largely sees Netflix as a platform that will let people be exposed to other cultures. At the same French media conference, he outlined that International Originals also mean more to him than just creating new TV shows and movies. 'We're very ambitious about being a positive force of people understanding other cultures through series and cinema,' he said. Because Netflix is available in virtually every country and making its shows watchable in multiple languages, it allows people to be exposed to things they wouldn't normally experience. It's a small gesture but, within an increasingly divided political landscape, it can be worthy.

'When I watch Russian movies, it's the closest I ever get to modern Russia,' he told the Utah Technology Council in 2018. 'I watch a bunch of Russian movies and I start to understand a lot more about Russia that otherwise is a very alien society to me. I'm a big believer in entertainment for connecting the world, creating empathy around the world and how powerful that is for solving some of our biggest problems.'[18]

A large amount of original content – from anywhere in the world – means Netflix can fill its catalogue with its own shows, rather than having to negotiate expensive licensing deals in every country. However, it does run the risk of leaving the platform without already established big-name titles that continue to be popular with viewers.

'As a result of our success with original content, we're becoming less focused on second run programming,' the company said in a letter to shareholders in early 2019.[19] But there are still some marquee shows that help to keep users coming back. The same letter said the company was willing to pay 'top-of-market prices' when streaming rights are put up for sale by studios, producers and TV networks. It proved this when it spent a reported $100m to keep all ten series of *Friends* in its library during 2019.

As the development of Netflix Originals progresses, the company will become more savvy about how it handles their rights too and how it markets them. Hastings has speculated, and it may just be pure grandstanding, that in the long term he would love to see Netflix content in theme parks. He values the importance of having his own shows that are easily recognisable and can make money outside Netflix.

'Licensing and merchandising, though, that's a big one for us,' the CEO said seconds after he spoke about theme parks. There's been no bigger example of this than the second and third seasons of *Stranger Things*. During its marketing of both series Netflix created *Stranger Things*-branded trainers with Reebok and Nike, took over the Oxford Street store of the UK clothes brand Topshop, partnered with Coca-Cola for 'New Coke' references, added the Upside Down to the hit game *Fortnite* and launched a huge partnership with Microsoft around a rerelease of its original Windows 1 operating system.[20]

Hastings knows the value of having large brand-name shows and it's something the company is keen to exploit. A 2017 job advertisement called for someone to lead the licensing of its efforts across areas such as books, comics, gaming, toys and clothing. Towards the end of the following year, Christie Fleischer joined from Disney, where she was the head of merchandise for its theme parks and the merchandise it sells.

And as the company's strategy on licensing grows, expect it to protect the intellectual property that proves valuable. When an unlicensed *Stranger Things*-themed pop-up bar appeared in Chicago ahead of the second season's launch, Netflix lawyers sent a cease-and-desist letter.

'Look, I don't want you to think I'm a total wastoid, and I love how much you guys love the show. (Just wait until you see Season 2.) But unless I'm living in the Upside Down, I don't think we did a deal with you for this pop-up,' the carefully crafted message said. The bar could keep running for the six weeks it had planned, but in future the company behind it should get in touch with Netflix first. It said: 'You're obviously creative types, so I'm sure you can appreciate that it's important to us to have a say in how our fans encounter the worlds we build.'[21]

9

BUILDING AN EDUCATION EMPIRE

Michael Kirst first heard of Reed Hastings after he sold Pure Software. 'He called me on the phone out of the blue and said he wanted to come to Stanford to study state education policy and that I was the professor who appeared to fit his needs,' Kirst, a professor emeritus of education and business administration at Stanford University, says in an interview.

And that's exactly what Hastings did. After selling his company for millions of dollars he enrolled at the Stanford Graduate School of Education to study for a master's degree in education policy. Kirst says he completed the first two semesters but then started to become distracted by political education campaigns, which he worked on and as a result didn't finish his second Stanford degree.

Learning has always piqued Hastings's interest. During

his time at Bowdoin College, where he earned his initial diploma, he took a proactive role in the parts of maths classes where students were responsible for helping to teach each other. He took time to 'explain basic concepts to the average student in ways they could understand', his former maths professor Bill Barker said in an interview with the college's newspaper in 2013.[1] Barker explained that Hastings then went on to write a detailed proposal of how the self-taught elements of the course could be reworked. It was the first time a student had ever done this.

Hastings's interest in how people learn continued during the years he was teaching maths in Eswatini, the southern African country formerly known as Swaziland. 'If I ever do go the grad school/professor route I know I would be much more into teaching, inspiring and developing the students, than my own research,' he wrote in a letter to Barker at the time.

But it wasn't until after he'd made his first fortune by selling Pure that his thoughts turned to the idea of philanthropy and using his money for something useful. 'After Pure Software, I had a bunch of money, and I didn't really want to buy yachts and such things,' he told the *Wall Street Journal* in 2008.[2]

The money posed a problem as there were plenty of different places that it could be used. 'One of the keys is saying, which problem do I want to work on?' Hastings told the Utah Technology Council in a talk in October 2018. The environment, human rights and healthcare, as well as many other areas, could appeal to a newly created multimillionaire. Whatever Hastings decided to pick, he knew that any change would be slow. 'We have to have patience, we have to support each other because there are very few problems that can be fixed in five years and the ones we have are big, hard ones,' Hastings said in the talk.

Ultimately, education was the option. 'For me, I chose education because the Peace Corps assigned me to be a teacher,' he said. 'If the Peace Corps had assigned me to be a fish farmer I'd probably be working in aquaculture now. It's just the thing that I knew a little bit about from two years in the classroom.'[3]

The earlier years of his education work were focused on the politics of education. In 1998 he helped write a law that would repeal a cap on the number of charter schools that could open in California each year. ('What charters are about is a mandate for change in the entire district,' Hastings said at the time.[4]) Hastings spent $3.3m of his own money in California to promote the issues of charter schools and ultimately get support for the bonds issue, the *Los Angeles Times* reported in 1999.[5]

He told the paper he was spending large sums of money because he wanted to change education. 'We've all succeeded because of our education, and we want to make sure that all Americans at least have a fair shot at that education,' he said, before adding that he was giving money to candidates '70 per cent based on relationship and 30 per cent on policy'. Some of his donations were made to Republican political candidates, despite his being a Democrat.

This initial move into education politics was followed

in 2000 by working on a campaign, called Proposition 39, which saw the state's education law changed. Hastings donated $1m to the campaign, which passed and reduced the percentage of votes needed from authorities to approve school funding.

As Netflix was showing signs that it could survive in 2000 and the first thoughts of an IPO were taking place, Hastings took on another role. In February that year, at the age of 39, he was appointed to the California State Board of Education by the Democrat governor, Gray Davis. (Before his appointment to the board Hastings had also served on an informal panel for Davis to help advise on education policy.) This saw Hastings take the lead on education policy for millions of children across California. 'He used his money and influence to be close to Governor Gray Davis, and he appointed him to the State Board of Education and his colleagues elected him president,' Kirst says.

Hastings sat as the board's president until 2004, when his first term on the panel was up. In her book, *Netflixed*, Gina Keating wrote that Hastings taking the role on the board surprised staff at Netflix and saw the company remove softcore pornography from its DVD collection, as Hastings feared the titles wouldn't do his new position any favours with rivals.

During this time he helped to change some rules concerning charter schools, oversaw rule changes to do with school safety, and faced protests about a high-school exit exam that critics thought was too difficult and saw too many students fail. At one point in 2001 Hastings was criticised for giving a senator $50,000 to help with their work, a day after they had passed laws that would benefit charter schools.

Despite this, Kirst remembers Hastings as being effective in the role. He explains that during his time on the education board Hastings would call upon him – he has served in the same president role for four terms – and other Stanford professors for advice. Kirst says: 'He would send me and others long emails where he did analyses of all kinds of education data like correlations between school achievement and various interventions and say: "Does this look right to you?"'

Within these emails would be 'long tables of complex numbers' and analysis, Kirst adds. He says Hastings clearly spent a lot of time looking at the details and intricacies of policy decisions and studies that were taking place. Kirst likens Hastings's approach to studying the finer details of the education world to the meticulous approach of his background in computer science.

'He applied these technical skills that he had as an engineer and a well-educated person that knew how to manipulate numbers,' he says. 'It is pretty extraordinary to have a major business executive taking time off to study education full-time, and then while he's leading Netflix he's sending these educational analyses to people and having respect for people who have studied education, policy change and improvement over a long period of time.'

Despite the inevitable political criticisms Hastings faced

during his first term on the board, he was put up for reappointment in 2004 when Arnold Schwarzenegger became the state's Republican governor. However, this time he wasn't set to become president and his role on the board would end just a year later. He left the board after political in-fighting.

At the start of January 2005, Hastings had to appear in front of the Senate Rules Committee and face a vote of approval amid criticism of one of the policies he implemented in his time as president of the education board. The board decided that students being taught in Spanish in bilingual classrooms should have half of their day – around two and a half hours – being taught in English.

Critics of the plans said the board had exceeded its authority in introducing the policy and that not enough materials for helping students learn English had been provided. They eventually won and he lost the crucial vote. At the time newspaper reports said Hastings's defeat in the Senate was largely about Democratic Party politics rather than Schwarzenegger being a Republican governor. The defeat was the first time that a nominee of Schwarzenegger had been publicly dismissed. Yet, after the loss, the governor still supported Hastings's work. A spokesperson for Schwarzenegger told the *Los Angeles Times*: 'What signal do you send to parents and children when a qualified and well-respected community leader like Reed Hastings is sacrificed to advocates of a narrowly focused agenda who wield power in Sacramento?'[6]

With the vote, Hastings's time on the education board

was over. However, he had learnt important lessons about how politics works and the importance of school funding, which would be useful as he shifted more into philanthropy and backing education technology firms.

He's not the only US billionaire from Silicon Valley to have proposed ideas for ways to fix the US education system. Mark Zuckerberg, Bill Gates and Elon Musk, plus plenty of other tech luminaries, have at various points suggested how schools, colleges and universities could be changed for a way they believe is better.

During his years in education Kirst says he's met a lot of leaders from big US businesses who want to fix schooling. Most of the time, he says, they believe they can reform education because they've been successful in business. But in reality they don't properly understand the complexities of the system.

'Hastings was the reverse of that,' Kirst explains. 'He was very humble and said: "I know this is complex and I need to really study it and learn from some professors and read deeply on how to change this." And that's just a refreshing attitude that enabled him to be effective and to continue to be a leader in education policy.'

Bringing algorithms to education

Hastings's big educational focus has been the expansion of charter schools across the United States. In the US, charter schools are public schools that must follow state and federal regulations. The majority of these schools are non-profits, but some exist as profit-making enterprises. They provide an alternative option to other public schools, and because of the way they are set up can offer different forms of structure, governance and use of technology.

The big appeal of the schools for Hastings is how they can be managed. In 2014 he told the California Charter Schools Association that he supported the school type as, unlike local US school boards, they don't have elections to decide who sits on the boards. He argues that the schools can be more stable because they don't have rotating boards that regularly change how they're run and who the super-intendents are.

'The importance of the charter school movement is to evolve America from a system where governance is con-stantly changing and you can't do long-term planning to a system of large non-profits that are great at professional development and training,' Hastings told the conference.[7]

Schools should be run, in some ways, like businesses, Hastings argues. Within companies, the board that over-sees how decisions are made doesn't change on a regular basis and is able to plan for the future. 'We need a lot more variety in the system and a lot more educator-centric organisations,' he said during a 2018 TED Talk, adding that he believes non-profit schools can be 'more mission focused, they support the educators well'.[8]

The issue of charter schools is a complex one. In some areas they have worked, in others they've not. Proponents of education boards have argued that local government, including that of schools, is key to the US democracy. 'If Mr. Hastings thinks local school boards should be replaced, does he also believe that we should get rid of all other locally elected bodies, including city councils and county boards of supervisors?' was part of the response from the California School Board Association to Hastings's 2014 speech.[9]

Hastings has been consistent in his support of charter schools. The idea that there should be a layer of democracy removed from the school system is likely to be a controversial one for a long time to come. He's advocated the idea that if the number of charter schools is going to grow and their percentage of students is to increase, then there needs to be slow but consistent progress. 'We have to have the steady discipline of every year more schools, better funding, better facilities access, more freedom. It's a lot of hard, steady work,' he said in 2014.

Hastings is on the board of directors of the Knowledge is Power Program (KIPP) – the largest network for charter schools in the United States. He has also in 2015 donated $2m to the non-profit Rocketship Public Schools, which is a network of charter schools that uses technology to help teachers with tuition. Previously, he funded academic studies that analyse students' grades.

Aside from charter schools, there's one other area that Hastings is involved in: bringing more technology to education. These efforts are slightly less surprising than his attempts to reform the structure of school boards and local education systems entirely.

Much like the efforts at Netflix, Hastings is interested in

how personalisation technologies can change how children learn. 'The hardest thing that many teachers face is the classroom of 30,' *Forbes* reported Hastings saying at a conference in 2012.[10] He explained that from his time teaching in Eswatini decades before, very little had changed to help teachers who had to deal with a large range of abilities.

'You'd have five kids who could barely do fractions. Five kids who were pushing the bounds of algebra. And then you'd have 20 kids in the middle. So, you taught to the middle, and you tried to work a little bit with each group,' he said. 'You always felt, "I'm not quite doing the right thing." You tried to make it up with sessions outside the classroom. It was just hard and inefficient.'

He believes the way to fix the issue of teaching resources and different abilities is 'individualised instruction'. This can come from a technological source, he argues. As well as the Rocketship schools he's invested in, Hastings has also heavily backed a tech system called DreamBox Learning.

DreamBox teaches maths through its software and personalises lessons for students based on their abilities and performance. Like Netflix, it collects a huge amount of data about how it's used and then tailors the lessons based on what it has learnt about a pupil. The system collects 50,000 data points per student each hour. These include whether the answer was correct, every click that's made, where hesitations happen and, of course, where mistakes are made.

'It is probably fair to say I recognised the power of personalisation maybe more than other people, because I had seen it in my own working life,' Hastings told the *New York Times* in 2017.[11] Having this much data about how students perform allows the lessons DreamBox offers to be tweaked to each individual. It knows where a student's knowledge is both strong and weak and as a result it can aim to help them improve by focusing on areas where more practice and learning are needed. The lessons, which go from US kindergarten level to the eighth grade, can take the shape of games and, when they are completed, children earn points that can be used to unlock rewards within the software.

Hastings first became interested in DreamBox around 2010. That year he and the non-profit group the Charter School Growth Fund invested $10m in the company. In a release announcing the funding Hastings said DreamBox had the 'best underlying adaptive technology' of any education platform he had seen. This was followed up in 2013 with a further combined investment of $14.5m with three other investors. In August 2018 the company raised $130m in investment to help it expand to more schools and countries around the world. (At the time of the investment it said almost three million students use its tech and it was being used across all 50 US states.)

As well as working with companies to expand the reach of charter schools, Hastings has also given his money away through philanthropy. In 2012 he joined the Giving Pledge, which was created by Bill and Melinda Gates and Warren Buffett. The Giving Pledge started in August 2010: 40 of the richest families in the US committed to the pledge, which would see them promise to give away more than half of their overall wealth. Since then billionaires including Tesla and SpaceX boss Elon Musk; Carl Icahn, the investor who was heavily involved with Blockbuster; and Sheryl Sandberg, the chief operating officer of Facebook, have signed up. (The Giving Pledge has now expanded to more than 189 billionaires from 22 countries around the world.)

A statement from Hastings and his wife, Patty Quillin, said they were 'thrilled to join with other fortunate people to pledge a majority of our assets to be invested in others'.[12] The pledge doesn't dictate how the billionaires have to spend their money, just that they will do so. The announcement added that Hastings and Quillin were already actively involved in the education space.

In January 2016, around the same time as Netflix had announced it was expanding its streaming in 130 countries around the world, Hastings had his own personal announcement to make. 'I'm thrilled to announce that I'm funding a new $100 million philanthropic fund for education, creatively named the Hastings Fund, through the Silicon Valley Community Foundation,' he posted on Facebook.[13] The fund, which would be managed by its own CEO, would donate an initial total of $1.5m to help fund college education for black and Latino students.

In response to the status update, Facebook's Mark Zuckerberg replied thanking Hastings for this 'leadership on education'. The reply said: 'You've been an important mentor and example for me and Cilla, and we look forward to working together even more.'

10

NETFLIX'S NEXT DECADE

Frosties or Sugar Puffs? It's the seemingly inconsequential decision faced by Stefan, a budding game designer living in London during the 1980s. But for Netflix viewers it was just the beginning of a huge technological development.

The choice comes at the start of 'Bandersnatch' – an interactive episode of the dark dystopian thriller *Black Mirror*. Viewers (or players) are presented with Stefan's story and every few minutes are given a series of options as to what happens next. The episode was first made available to the almost 200 countries that Netflix operates in, with their more than 130 million subscribers, on 28 December 2018. Within hours, the choose-your-own-adventure-style TV show had gone viral.

More than five hours of video footage were recorded for 'Bandersnatch', which is divided into 250 individual segments. The parts users see are dependent on the either/ or choices they make using their remotes or on-screen taps during the show, and it means there's a hugely intricate web of different versions of 'Bandersnatch' that the watcher could eventually see on their ultimate journey to one of five different endings.

To produce the episode, Netflix's engineers created their own software that allows for the individual segments to be easily streamed, avoiding any buffering from taking place. The single film took almost a year to produce but was one of the biggest technological undertakings completed by Netflix since it started streaming in 2007 and then rolled out to the rest of the world in 2016.

Hastings – who said 73 per cent of people picked Frosties in a January 2019 earnings call – has emphasised that the future for Netflix involves more experimentation. It has since followed up 'Bandersnatch' with more interactive shows – although, in typical fashion, it hasn't revealed how many people watched the special episode of *Black Mirror*. In the short term, over the coming years it's likely that Hastings and the firm will try other experiments with storytelling. There will be repeats of the format that created 'Bandersnatch', but the teams will undoubtedly use the technology to trial other forms of interactivity. This could be something as simple as shows in which voting takes place, more control could be given to users through their remotes, and other forms of development.

But Netflix wants to be around for more than the short term. Hastings wants the business to survive another 20 years at least. Netflix's future exists on a number of different fronts: subscriber growth and its revenues, the content it makes and the competition it faces. All three are closely linked, with each having an impact on what the company can achieve elsewhere.

The company's growth in the US has largely stalled – although there is still some room for expansion, it has high penetration rates across the country – and it's now reliant on adding new subscribers from outside of the US. There have been more non-US subscribers than US-based subscribers since July 2017. As the company moves forward it will increasingly need to take a more international approach to keep the number of new subscribers growing.

Because Netflix is based in California and spent its first decade as a United States only service, it is inevitably seen through the lens of an American media company. This isn't a surprise: its investors are largely US-based, it sits on the American stock markets, and large amounts of its salaried workforce are in the country. (Hollywood being US-based also aids with how Netflix is seen.)

Given the company's existing tactic of licensing its Original shows to China, it is unlikely that any deal will be struck with the government to create a Netflix subsidiary within the state. This means Netflix's biggest single market growth opportunity is India – the world's second-largest nation.

Cracking India will be difficult. It may even be impossible. The Bollywood film industry is rich in content and quantity. To cut through the noise of the thousands of films released in the country every year, Netflix needs to make its offerings stand out. It has the budget to promote its own titles, but the storytelling also needs to reverberate with viewers. The country has an increasing level of internet penetration, yet there are high levels of poverty and sensitivities to pricing. Netflix has been making strides with its original content in India, having produced a number of local films. Next it will have to hyperlocalise the content it's making: moving into regional dialects.

However, as it invests in more original programming from outside America and its international subscriber base eventually becomes double that of its domestic one, it would make sense for Hastings to position Netflix differently. There needs to be less of a focus on America and more effort dedicated to other countries around the world. This could include building more teams of engineers outside the US and making sure local markets have the right number of staff working in them.

For more international growth Netflix has to have people working near to where its customers live. Subscribers won't be satisfied with slow customer service answers when staff work in different time zones, and they need to be able to pay in ways that are easy and convenient to them. The price also needs to work for each country Netflix is in. Outside high-GDP countries, Netflix may struggle to attract significant market penetration with its current roughly one-size-fits-all pricing structure. For instance, in an effort to reach a mass population in India, Hastings launched a mobile-only version of Netflix in July 2019. Unlike its regular app, it is a cut-price offering, costing just $3.63 for a monthly subscription.

Originals have been a huge focus for Netflix since *House of Cards* took the world by storm in 2013. The company didn't know if the $100m it paid for the series would be worth it. It was a gamble that could have crippled the firm. Ultimately, the show was a hit and launched Netflix's ambitious plans for the original shows it has.

Since then, Netflix has produced and bankrolled hundreds of Originals – while also slapping its Originals label on shows it has paid for the exclusive rights to. This will continue and at a greater scale. The company is set to produce more Original shows in a greater selection of countries. These Originals will be marketed highly in their local markets, but the company will also look for them to be successful internationally. It is increasing the amount of languages it makes shows available in, so they'll be viewed in as many different places as possible.

There's no hint that Hastings is going to move into other forms of television. He's always denied that Netflix would start showing any types of live sports. Its documentaries cover stories about sport but not actual matches, races or events themselves. The view of Hastings has been that the company can't do anything to differentiate any sports coverage from that of its competitors. (Amazon Prime has moved into live sporting events, buying rights for UK Premier League football matches as well as NFL matches and live tennis events from around the world.) It's roughly the same approach for news coverage too. (Netflix did experiment with a news-related talk show hosted by a comedian, Chelsea Handler, but it was cancelled after two seasons.)

There's one area of traditional TV that Netflix has moved into. It has vastly upped its production of unscripted reality television. *Tidying Up with Marie Kondo* and the remake of *Queer Eye for the Straight Guy* are its stalwarts of the genre. These unscripted shows are unlikely to cost as much as elaborate big-budget series, will follow a straightforward format, and will create human connections with the viewers.

What will be key for Netflix's success with movies and TV shows is how much of a buzz they create. The company cannot bankroll a majority of shows that don't help to drive new subscribers. Huge hits which are viewed by millions of people – such as *Orange Is the New Black*, *Stranger Things* and *Bird Box* – help to raise the profile of Netflix. The programmes can only be seen on its service as it has the exclusive rights to them, and if customers want to watch, then they have to sign up. Compelling stories that extend beyond Netflix subscribers to the awareness of non-subscribers is an effective way to increase how many people pay each month.

The other big way Netflix can attract new subscribers, out of its generally younger millennial appeal, is by striking deals with existing service providers. Across Europe, Hastings has partnered with the Rupert Murdoch-owned Sky Television to include Netflix as part of some of its more expensive packages. Netflix shows are folded into its electronic programming guide and customers can easily join without having to create separate accounts. In the US, Netflix has made a similar deal with Comcast to allow its shows to be watched through an account with the telecoms company.

Traditionally these companies would be seen as competitors, but now Netflix has reached such a huge scale there are benefits to each party in having Netflix available. Service providers can incorporate more original shows from Netflix that their customers may be talking about or have heard of, and Netflix is able to reach a demographic that it may not have been able to do without the partnership.

Hastings has always had competition. Walmart, Blockbuster, Redbox, Amazon and more have all offered direct competing services throughout his 20 years at the helm of the company. There have also been the offerings of traditional TV and movie studios (HBO, Hulu and more). Analysts have almost always not backed Netflix; the company's share price has fluctuated wildly over the last two decades and most of the time the changes have been as a result of what its competition has been doing.

Yet Netflix has endured. Historically, Blockbuster was its biggest threat but a combination of Hastings's early lead, better technology and Blockbuster's financial troubles led to Netflix being victorious. In recent years nobody has been able to dethrone the business from its dominant market position. That could change in the decade up to 2030 as the competitive threat to Netflix is greater than ever before.

Amazon appears to be attempting to do everything with its Prime Video service – which is tagged on to its Prime delivery service. Within Prime Video, sports are included as well as original TV and movies plus those Amazon has the licence to stream. Showing the depths of its financial pockets, the company has reportedly spent $250m on the rights to produce five seasons of a *Lord of the Rings* prequel.

Amazon also has pay-per-view where a huge library of individual titles can be rented for one-off payments. Amazon Prime has scaled with more than 100 million paid members around the world. It's not clear how many of them watch Prime Video, but Jeff Bezos has said that in 2017 it secured the rights to more than 3,000 films and that 'Prime Video continues to drive Prime member adoption and retention'.[1]

Apple, given its ginormous iPhone, Mac and iPad user base, may be able to make quick gains on Netflix. Its subscription video service is Apple TV+, and the company spent big on acquiring stars for its shows: Oprah Winfrey, Steven Spielberg, Jennifer Aniston, Reese Witherspoon and J.J. Abrams are all involved. Amid declining iPhone sales, and billions being spent on content, there's the potential for Apple's streaming service to be an almost instant success. Through iTunes it has the technological ability to create a streaming service that uses personalisation and recommendation systems to get people interested in its shows.

It is starting from scratch with its own original content and will have to build up the infrastructure to ensure the shows are produced. The struggle for Apple, though, will be creating shows that people want to watch. Traditionally Apple has been a conservative technology company, which presents itself as being very family friendly and largely risk-averse when it comes to sensitive issues. While its roster of celebrities is impressive, the biggest question is whether Apple will introduce enough gritty content to convince subscribers to stick with it. Like Amazon, Apple has been hiring plenty of former studio executives to run its divisions, and both companies have the billions required to aggressively pursue their streaming services.

In contrast, Disney will have a good shot at disrupting Netflix's growth from a film and series point of view. In creating its Disney+ streaming subscription service, the company has pulled its shows from Netflix, with jointly produced Marvel Universe series (*Daredevil*, *Jessica Jones* and more) not being renewed. The company may be a content powerhouse and creating new original shows from its *Star Wars*, Marvel and other franchises, but it's a long way behind in terms of technology and customers.

It's unlikely that Disney+ will seriously challenge Netflix on subscriber numbers for several years, though. Hastings had a 150-million-plus subscriber starting point. While Disney will inevitably draw some people away from Netflix, a mass exodus from Netflix and swelling of Disney subscribers won't be instant. It's likely Disney's and Apple's growth will be more methodical and they will catch up with Netflix over time. Although some worrying signs were seen for Netflix in July 2019, when its US subscriber numbers dropped for the first time since the Qwikster incident. It lost 130,000 US subscribers during the second quarter of the year and only added 2.7 million new global subscribers, well below the five million it had forecast. Hastings blamed the company's price rise, and a lack of blockbuster Original shows being released over the three months.

What's likely, though, is that all of the streaming services will have their place. The UK's public service broadcasters, the BBC and ITV, have created their own paid subscription service to host their own content on. People will subscribe to some combination of Netflix, Disney+, Amazon Prime, Apple's offering, Hulu, plus traditional linear television and their own streaming and on-demand options. (YouTube is also increasingly focusing some of its efforts on produced shows rather than just user-generated and user-uploaded raw footage.) Each service will be competing for people's time and attempting to attract their attention, but it's unlikely that one service will dominate the market to a point where others can't survive. There will be some losses but Disney, Netflix, Amazon and Apple all have the bankrolls to keep their efforts afloat.

One advantage that Netflix has in its favour is the fact it does only one thing. Hastings has kept the company focused on subscriptions and streaming TV shows, movies and documentaries. It would have been easy to attempt to move the company into new areas. Hastings could have easily started renting games – in the company's early years and during Qwikster it was mentioned but never materialised. It could also have pivoted to virtual reality. His decision not to move into hardware was also correct; the company would have been distracted by something it couldn't excel at and would eventually be irrelevant with the emergence of internet-connected TVs and smartphones everywhere.

The big bet is Netflix's Original shows. In coming up towards a decade that it has been making them, Sarandos, the chief content officer, has started to create franchises. *Orange Is the New Black*, *Stranger Things* and others have an almost cult-like status among fans. And they can only be watched on Netflix. If people think they're missing out on great TV and movies that their friends and family are watching, then they'll pay for Netflix.

While subjective, Netflix Originals don't have the gravitational pull of Disney's Marvel or *Star Wars* franchises, or the history of *Mission Impossible*, or the success of DC's *Batman* titles. But the company's aim is to turn its shows and movies into titles with the same must-watch reputation.

'People will get crowded out if they don't do good shows,' Hastings told the *New York Times*'s DealBook conference in 2015. 'If you get obsessed by other people and don't focus on getting great content then you can lose.'[2]

There's no doubt that Hastings has reinvented how people watch television and redefined entertainment – it invented binge-watching. It may not have killed traditional TV viewing, but in the Western world for many people Netflix is TV. It's a place where they first turn to for an evening's entertainment. Within the industry Netflix has become the company that competitors want to emulate, it's the driving force in the online TV marketplace, and for now it has the power. The company has huge buying force, has created a strong technological underpinning, and built up a cult status.

At the centre of it all, Hastings has tried to keep the fact that Netflix is a movie company in some sort of perspective. 'When I look at the challenges that Gandhi had, or the various leaders through history, our challenges pale in comparison to this,' he said in an interview with *Vanity Fair* in 2012 while talking about the Qwikster episode that nearly killed the company. 'Over the last 10 years, I've read a ton about Winston Churchill and Abraham Lincoln. I've worked very hard, but my life's always been fun. It's not been the Civil War of 1862. That was dark, and how you hold things together at a time like that is completely different than what we experienced.'[3]

But he is aware that if how people are entertained radically changes, then Netflix's future may change. 'At some point new forms of entertainment will supplant movies and TV shows and then Netflix will have a threat,' Hastings said at a *New Yorker* conference in 2016. 'If that threat is digitally based, it's something you do on a screen, then we've got a pretty good chance of being able to figure that out as a similar skill set. But to the degree that the substitute for what we offer is pharmacological and you take a little blue pill that's very personalised medicine and you have an incredible movie in your head and whenever you want you take a white pill that brings you right back then it's unlikely that we'll be successful in pioneering that new format.'[4]

EPILOGUE

EPILOGUE

On 12 November 2019, a sleeping giant stuttered into life. The date marked the first time Disney+, the streaming service of the Walt Disney Company, became available for users living in the United States. On day one there were around 7,500 television episodes and more than 500 movies available to subscribers. These included classic Disney titles and newly commissioned productions.

While the launch was hotly anticipated, it was not without flaws. As people flocked to join the service early in the morning, they were greeted with error messages. 'Unable to connect to Disney+,' the message read. 'There seems to be an issue connecting to the Disney+ service. Please try again later if the issue persists.'

In response to the technical problems the company was forced to issue a statement. A spokesperson for the company said the demand for Disney+ had 'exceeded our high expectations' and it was working hard to fix the $6.99 per month service. (A price that undercuts Hastings's most affordable plan.) Within days of the launch there was another issue: thousands of account usernames and passwords were found to have been circulated for free, or a small cost, on hacking forums around the world.

Despite early teething issues, Disney+'s launch will have made Hastings pay attention. Disney announced that its first day in the US had seen it reach 10 million signups. Later third-party analysis said that within the first few weeks more than 22 million people had downloaded the app on mobile devices. The research, conducted by Apptopia, said during the first four weeks of its public availability, people in the US had spent 200 million hours using the app. The figure for Netflix, which has vastly more subscribers, was one billion hours.

Google also cemented Disney+'s popularity among US consumers. The company's annual analysis of the top trending search terms said Disney+ came out on top. This doesn't mean that Americans searched for Disney+ more than anything else, but it was the most popular search term when they're ranked by an increase in popularity.

These were the opening salvos in what will become a long streaming war. By the time this book is published, Disney will be rolling its streaming services out to large chunks of Europe and it will be possible to see what impact, if any, this has on Netflix. Analysts from Wedbush Securities have said Disney could hit its initial 60-90 million subscriber target by 2022, two years earlier than the previously planned 2024.

In the world of entertainment, the decade of 2020 to 2030 will mark the streaming wars. It will also be Netflix's third decade of existence. Netflix's dominant position won't see it caught quickly, but there's the potential that Disney will start to make significant gains on the service. This is a battle that will be fought around the world – the US will be a key market, but not the only one. (Netflix has pledged to spend $400 million on new productions in India during 2020 and is lowering its prices in the country to draw in more subscribers.)

Throughout its first two decades, Netflix has faced battles that have repeated themselves. It struggled with a lack of DVD player owners (then slow rollout of broadband speeds), movie studios weren't happy with it renting DVDs as they went on sale (then they also butted against the company for online streaming rights) and the Blockbuster price battle was emulated by Netflix and HBO and Hulu's early streaming battles. During this time, Hastings has proven that TV streamed across the internet is a business model that works. People want to watch shows at their convenience and aren't reliant on traditional linear scheduling.

But it's unlikely the streaming market will be a winner-takes-all environment. Consumers are likely to subscribe to multiple platforms, but only the ones they keep finding things to watch on. The streaming wars will be as much about the films and TV shows the companies involved make as much as the number of subscribers they have. If Disney+ rockets in front of Netflix in terms of subscribers, but they spend less time watching its shows, who is the real winner?

The company's third decade will be defined by how well it copes with its rivals upping their game. The challenges it will face will echo those from its DVD and early streaming days, but this time, the rivals are bigger. Netflix's main competitors are now established entertainment and technology companies that have multiple strands to their business.

Hastings knows this. Ahead of Disney+'s launch he said he wasn't 'worried' about the service but acknowledged the streaming platform is one of his biggest rivals already. 'They're a wonderful competitor, because they really understand creativity,' he said at the *New York Times'* DealBook conference in November 2019. He said he would be subscribing to the service when it launched. 'Disney's the one that we really have the most to learn from in terms of entertainment.'

ACKNOWLEDGEMENTS

Huge shifts in the entertainment industry only occur every couple of decades. Colour TV displays slowly displaced black-and-white monitors, digital signals eventually took the place of analogue ones and the DVD finally overtook VHS tapes. The generation of streaming movies and TV shows over the internet is still relatively new.

In the months I spent writing this book, Netflix's dominance has started to be challenged. When I started the process Disney+ and Apple TV+ were internal projects at the world's leading media and technology companies. Now they are a reality, with people watching their shows all around the world.

Who will win the streaming industry – if any single company actually can – remains to be seen. The coming weeks, months and years will show if Netflix has the sticking power and experience to swat away its rivals. However, throughout the process of writing this book, I have been indebted to the people who have provided their expertise.

A huge amount of thanks is owed to all the former Netflix staff who took the time to speak to me, share their wisdom and recount their memories of Reed and of working at the firm. Many of them are named throughout this book but there are others, and those who haven't worked at Netflix, who provided background information, confirmed what happened and generally brought the book together.

Thank you to the editors and staff at Orion Books and Weidenfeld & Nicolson for commissioning the book, in particular Paul Murphy, who drove its direction. Finally, a huge amount of gratitude is needed for my family and partner Stephanie, who had to hear plenty of complaints about the structuring, sourcing and writing process of the entire manuscript. They all made it possible.

REFERENCES

1. CAN ANYONE BEAT REED HASTINGS?

1. https://www.wired.com/2002/12/netflix-6/

2. REED HASTINGS JR

1. https://www.nytimes.com/1975/08/12/archives/alfred-lee-loomis-dead-at-87-physicist-financier-and-lawyer.html
2. https://www.newyorker.com/magazine/2014/02/03/outside-the-box-2
3. https://www.vanityfair.com/news/2012/02/netflix-201202
4. https://www.cnbc.com/2017/10/17/netflix-reed-hastings-joins-forbes-400-list-for-the-first-time.html
5. https://www.bloomberg.com/billionaires/profiles/reed-hastings/

6. https://www.youtube.com/watch?v=vI-Vphpk2WY&

7. https://www.nytimes.com/2006/12/17/jobs/17boss.html

8. http://bowdoinorient.com/bonus/article/8535

9. https://www.educationnext.org/disrupting-the-education-monopoly-reed-hastings-interview/

10. http://bowdoinorient.com/bonus/article/8535

11. https://www.youtube.com/watch?v=BsXXIfqbnRk

12. https://www.nytimes.com/2006/12/17/jobs/17boss.html

13. https://thenextweb.com/entrepreneur/2013/09/12/inspiring-entrepreneurs-reed-hastings-netflix/

14. https://web.stanford.edu/class/cs343/resources/purify.pdf

15. https://books.google.co.uk/books?id=NwUAAAAAM-BAJ&pg=PA23&lpg=PA23&dq=Pure+Software+purify&source=bl&ots=i3wGiFgP5a&sig=ACfU3U2CriG-OrRG1oHDd4CUMkwNwyUO6Nw&hl=en&sa=X-&ved=2ahUKEwjj6dCD9czgAhXqQxUIHQvIC6gQ6A-EwCHoECBgQAQ#v=onepage&q=Pure%20Software%20purify&f=falsehttps://books.google.co.uk/books?id=NwUAAAAAMBAJ&pg=PA23&lpg=PA23&dq=Pure+Software+purify&source=bl&ots=i-3wGiFgP5a&sig=ACfU3U2CriGOrRG1oHDd4CUMk-wNwyUO6Nw&hl=en&sa=X&ved=2ahUKEwjj6d-CD9czgAhXqQxUIHQvIC6gQ6AEwCHoECB-gQAQ#v=onepage&q=Pure%20Software%20purify&f=false

16. https://www.forbes.com/global/1998/1102/0116070a.html#40c6f9e42c8d

17. https://www.youtube.com/watch?v=BsXXIfqbnRk

18. http://fortune.com/2010/11/18/

reed-hastings-leader-of-the-pack/

19. https://www.inc.com/magazine/20051201/qa-hastings.html

20. https://video.newyorker.com/watch/reed-hastings-on-inventing-the-future-of-television

21. https://venturebeat.com/2011/10/29/netflix-ceo-lessonsive-learnt-from-my-marriage-counsellor/

22. https://www.youtube.com/watch?v=BsXXIfqbnRk

23. http://fortune.com/2010/11/18/reed-hastings-leader-of-the-pack/

24. https://www.youtube.com/watch?v=Mzk-iL8KC9o

25. https://www.youtube.com/watch?v=BsXXIfqbnRk

3. THE BIRTH OF NETFLIX

1. https://www.nytimes.com/2006/12/17/jobs/17boss.html

2. https://www.bizjournals.com/sanjose/news/2014/01/08/netflixs-first-ceo-on-reed-hastings.html

3. https://www.bizjournals.com/sanjose/news/2014/01/08/netflixs-first-ceo-on-reed-hastings.html

4. https://hbr.org/2014/01/how-netflix-reinvented-hr

5. https://www.youtube.com/watch?v=jYhP08uuffs

6. Patty McCord, *Powerful: Building a Culture of Freedom and Responsibility* (Silicon Guild, 2018), p. 6

7. https://www.youtube.com/watch?v=Ad-jaovin3c

8. https://money.cnn.com/magazines/fsb/fsb_archive/2003/07/01/347314/

9. https://www.wsj.com/articles/SB984181374790463655

10. https://www.youtube.com/watch?v=BsXXIfqbnRk

11. https://hbr.org/2011/04/how-i-did-it-blockbusters-former-ceo-on-sparring-with-an-activist-shareholder

12. https://www.inc.com/magazine/20051201/qa-hastings.html

13. https://www.dallasnews.com/business/2010/05/08/Blockbuster-is-trying-to-turn-it-around

14. https://www.youtube.com/watch?v=pjsUsN1iLR0

15. https://hbr.org/2011/04/how-i-did-it-blockbusters-former-ceo-on-sparring-with-an-activist-shareholder

16. https://www.fool.com/investing/general/2008/12/10/blockbuster-ceo-has-answers.aspx

17. https://www.cbsnews.com/news/interview-blockbuster-ceo-dazed-and-confused-maybe-but-confident-of-physicals-digital-future/

18. https://www.latimes.com/archives/la-xpm-2010-apr-15-la-fi-ct-facetime15-2010apr15-story.html

19. https://www.fastcompany.com/1656502/blockbuster-ceo-jim-keyes-competition-apple-netflix-nintendo-and-redbox

20. https://www.youtube.com/watch?v=zCO0lNfs4oM

21. https://www.nytimes.com/2013/04/27/business/netflix-looks-back-on-its-near-death-spiral.html

4. A CULTURE OF FREEDOM

1. https://www.slideshare.net/reed2001/culture-1798664

2. https://www.gq.com/story/netflix-founder-reed-hastings-house-of-cards-arrested-development

3. https://www.businessinsider.com/netflix-ceo-reed-hastings-interview-2011-4?IR=T

4. https://jobs.netflix.com/culture
5. https://www.youtube.com/watch?v=BsXXIfqbnRk
6. https://www.mercurynews.com/2007/03/21/ at-netflix-vacation-time-has-no-limits/
7. https://www.youtube.com/watch?v=Ad-jaovin3c
8. https://www.wsj.com/articles/at-netflix-radical-transparency-and-blunt-firings-unsettle-the-ranks-1540497174
9. Patty McCord, *Powerful: Building a Culture of Freedom and Responsibility* (Silicon Guild, 2018), p. 139
10. https://twitter.com/jsf33/status/1010248478247694337
11. https://www.hollywoodreporter.com/live-feed/ jonathan-friedland-exits-netflix-1122675

5. INTERNET TV IS BORN

1. http://content.time.com/time/magazine/artcle/0,9171, 135245,00.html
2. http://fortune.com/2010/11/18/ reed-hastings-leader-of-the-pack/
3. https://money.cnn.com/2007/01/16/technology/netflix/
4. https://www.businessinsider.com/ netflix-ceo-reed-hastings-interview-2011-4?IR=T
5. https://latimesblogs.latimes.com/ entertainmentnewsbuzz/2011/09/netflix-offered-300-million-plus-but-starz-wanted-higher-prices.html
6. https://www.youtube.com/watch?v=7tWK0tW1fig
7. https://www.cnet.com/news/ netflix-ceo-i-slid-into-arrogance/

8. https://techcrunch.com/2011/09/19/the-guy-behind-the-qwikster-twitter-account-realizes-what-he-has-wants-a-mountain-of-cash/

9. https://www.nytimes.com/2011/10/25/technology/netflix-lost-800000-members-with-price-rise-and-split-plan.html

10. https://www.cnet.com/news/netflixs-lost-year-the-inside-story-of-the-price-hike-train-wreck/

11. https://mediadecoder.blogs.nytimes.com/2011/10/10/netflix-abandons-plan-to-rent-dvds-on-qwikster/

12. https://www.youtube.com/watch?v=0eAXW-zkGlM

6. DEALING IN DATA

1. https://www.youtube.com/watch?v=NgXxCs7UlQg

2. https://venturebeat.com/2016/01/18/netflixs-reed-hastings-says-decisions-on-programming-based-on-both-data-and-gut-instincts/

3. https://www.telegraph.co.uk/technology/2016/03/26/inside-netflix-how-reed-hastings-is-building-the-first-global-tv/

4. https://web.archive.org/web/20061011144855/https://www.netflixprize.com/

5. https://www.nytimes.com/2009/09/22/technology/internet/22netflix.html

6. https://www.wired.com/2007/12/why-anonymous-data-sometimes-isnt/

7. https://www.nytimes.com/2006/08/09/technology/09aol.html

8. https://www.wired.com/2010/03/netflix-cancels-contest/

9. https://www.youtube.com/watch?v=LsAN-TEJfN0

7. A CULTURE OF TRUST

1. https://www.youtube.com/watch?v=Mzk-iL8KC9o
2. https://www.slideshare.net/reed2001/culture-1798664
3. https://www.cnbc.com/2015/11/03/netflix-ceo-reed-hastings-why-i-take-6-weeks-vacation.html
4. https://www.youtube.com/watch?v=zCO0lNfs4oM
5. https://vimeo.com/158636592
6. Patty McCord, *Powerful: Building a Culture of Freedom and Responsibility* (Silicon Guild, 2018), p. 64
7. https://www.youtube.com/watch?v=LsAN-TEJfN0
8. https://www.youtube.com/watch?v=zCO0lNfs4oM
9. https://www.youtube.com/watch?v=jYhP08uuffs
10. https://www.nytimes.com/2017/08/08/technology/the-culture-wars-have-come-to-silicon-valley.html
11. https://www.youtube.com/watch?v=yD90x3RuyPY

8. GLOBAL DOMINANCE

1. https://www.youtube.com/watch?v=l5R3E6jsICA
2. https://www.fastcompany.com/1690905/netflix-ceo-apologizes-self-deprecating-humor-hints-streaming-only-service
3. https://www.wired.com/2016/01/the-counterintuitive-tech-behind-netflixs-worldwide-launch/
4. https://theintercept.com/collections/google-dragonfly-china/

5. https://www.recode.net/2016/1/6/11588564/netflix-ceo-reed-hastings-on-china-hbo-and-the-surprise-success-of

6. https://www.recode.net/2017/5/31/15720268/netflix-ceo-reed-hastings-net-neutrality-open-internet

7. https://media.netflix.com/en/press-releases/iqiyi-and-netflix-sign-licensing-agreement

8. https://www.youtube.com/watch?v=jYhP08uuffs

9. https://www.wired.com/2006/09/netflix-5/

10. https://www.hollywoodreporter.com/bastard-machine/review-lilyhammer-steven-van-zandt-sopranos-netflix-287367

11. https://www.youtube.com/watch?v=Mzk-iL8KC9o

12. https://www.vulture.com/2018/06/how-netflix-swallowed-tv-industry.html

13. https://www.youtube.com/watch?v=BsXXIfqbnRk

14. http://q4live.s22.clientfiles.s3-website-us-east-1.amazonaws.com/959853165/files/doc_financials/quartely_reports/2018/q3/NFLX-USQ_Transcript_2018-10-16.pdf

15. https://economictimes.indiatimes.com/small-biz/startups/newsbuzz/the-next-100-mn-users-of-netflix-will-come-from-india-netflix-ceo-reed-hastings/articleshow/63047513.cms

16. https://www.wired.co.uk/article/netflix-streaming-subscribers-business

17. https://www.youtube.com/watch?v=U1NHjEouVCw

18. https://www.youtube.com/watch?v=Ad-jaovin3c

19. https://s22.q4cdn.com/959853165/files/doc_financials/quarterly_reports/2019/q1/FINAL-Q119-Shareholder-Letter.pdf

20. https://variety.com/2019/biz/news/stranger-things-3-new-coke-ceo-1203263401/; https://bloody-disgusting.com/news/3571793/stranger-things-crossover-event-begun-fortnite/; https://arstechnica.com/gadgets/2019/07/microsofts-80s-throwback-turned-out-to-be-a-tie-in-for-stranger-things-3/

21. https://www.digitalspy.com/tv/ustv/a838517/netflix-cease-desist-letter-stranger-things-bar/

9. BUILDING AN EDUCATION EMPIRE

1. https://bowdoinorient.com/bonus/article/8535
2. https://www.wsj.com/articles/SB120251714532955425
3. https://www.youtube.com/watch?v=Ad-jaovin3c
4. https://www.latimes.com/archives/la-xpm-1998-may-08-mn-47633-story.html
5. https://www.latimes.com/archives/la-xpm-1999-apr-18-mn-28692-story.html
6. https://www.latimes.com/archives/la-xpm-2005-jan-13-me-hastings13-story.html
7. https://www.youtube.com/watch?v=iBMNllBviQU
8. https://www.youtube.com/watch?v=LsAN-TEJfN0
9. https://www.washingtonpost.com/news/answer-sheet/wp/2014/03/14/netflixs-reed-hastings-has-a-big-idea-kill-elected-school-boards/?utm_term=.e74d203bc438
10. https://www.forbes.com/sites/jamesmarshallcrotty/2012/05/03/netflix-ceo-reed-hastings-blew-12-billion-in-market-cap-so-why-should-we-listen-to-him-about-education/#2640009f41bb

11. https://www.nytimes.com/2017/06/06/technology/tech-billionaires-education-zuckerberg-facebook-hastings.html
12. https://money.cnn.com/2012/09/18/technology/reed-hastings-giving-pledge/
13. https://www.facebook.com/reed1960/posts/10153624015489584

10. NETFLIX'S NEXT DECADE

1. https://www.sec.gov/Archives/edgar/data/1018724/000119312518121161/d456916dex991.htm
2. https://www.youtube.com/watch?v=i-4Auh7vgDU
3. https://www.vanityfair.com/news/2012/02/netflix-201202
4. https://www.youtube.com/watch?v=yD90x3RuyPY

INDEX